Malice Cloaked in Liberty

The Killing of America

George Autry Jr.

Townhall Press
ON-DEMAND BOOK PUBLISHING FOR CONSERVATIVE AUTHORS

Malice Cloaked in Liberty
by George Autry Jr.
Published by Townhall Press

Printed in the United States of America

ISBN 978-1-60477-382-8

Unless otherwise indicated, Scripture is taken from the King James Version of the Bible.

www.townhallpress.com

Dedication

—⁓—

I t is my honor to dedicate this book to all the men and women who are daily waging war against those who would literally destroy our American way of life. To those talk show hosts, journalists, statesmen and stateswomen, and so many others who have placed the greater good of our nation over self, *you are* our homeland warriors.

Special Thanks

—ɯ—

O n behalf of all Americans who truly love our country, I wish to express a special thanks to Fox News and Bill O'Reilly. Fox News is a bright light cutting through the murky spin of the liberal media and others who would unashamedly distort truth and create a slanted version of events rather than report honestly.

Fox News has literally extended and may very well preserve the life of our nation for years to come. Bill O'Reilly, with his two-fisted, no-holds-barred quest for truth, has once again brought to the forefront the importance of absolute truth, not an admixture, while at the same time publicly chastising the merchants of deceit, lies, and venomous attacks on anything Christian, conservative, patriotic, and moral. America has received a wake-up call, for we have slumbered much too long.

Bill O'Reilly's challenge for the American people to stand up and be counted before we lose all that is precious and vital to us as a nation inspired me to write this book and to found the national organization America's Majority.

Bill O'Reilly is a true American hero.

I am grateful for the inspiration.

Purpose

—∿∿—

Uncloaking those who are killing America

Exposing who they are and how they are doing it

Proclaim liberty unto all the inhabitants thereof

throughout all the land . . .

—Leviticus 25:10

As free and not using your liberty for a cloak of maliciousness. . ..

—1 Peter 2:16

Foreword

—⟋⟍—

In many ways, George Autry Jr. is a modern-day Paul Revere. In his book *Malice Cloaked in Liberty,* he pleads with patriotic Americans to wake up, wake up, for the enemy is at our doorstep and has come to destroy our country and abolish our freedoms. Armed with truth and passion, George pointedly identifies these enemies and elaborates on their sinister intentions.

Should our beloved nation overcome this evil that is set before us, may we applaud George Autry and others for their vital roles. Should this great nation be buried in the graveyard of fallen empires, may we be forever shamed for sleeping through the cry to battle.

It is sad to be deaf and not hear, yet it is tragic to hear and not listen. God's plea echoes still today. Let us act upon what may be the final call.

Dr. Jim Palmer

Pastor and Noted Speaker

This compelling book exposes the hidden agendas that permeate so many organizations, religions, and people in our politically correct age. George Autry Jr.'s personal accounts and in-depth research make for an easy read as he gives us a true account of the causes of America's moral decay, corruption, and downward spiral. *Malice Cloaked in Liberty* is a must-read for all Americans who believe that standing up for America is the right thing to do.

Lieutenant Colonel Lacy A. Allen

Retired USAF

Contents

—⚋—

Introduction

During his storied and tumultuous reign as emperor of Rome, Julius Caesar was seen as the greatest leader ever in Roman history. His conquests of other peoples and lands took him to heights few had ever known. He was loved, feared, and hated. To draw a parallel, it was much like America today.

When certain members of the Roman Senate plotted to kill him, a plan was hatched for each senator to attend the Senate meeting with a dagger concealed in his cloak. Each senator was to plunge a dagger into Caesar, signifying that each would act independently to vent his hatred; yet by acting collectively, they could conceal the fact of whose dagger actually killed him.

Each dagger in its own way and placement took the life of Julius Caesar. When the deed was done, the senators fled in panic, none accepting responsibility or even remotely presenting a plan to preserve Roman life.

So it is with America today. Daggers are being wielded by individuals and organizations whose twisted hatred of democracy, decency, values, and morals has been and is being plunged into the life of our nation. Just as surely as Julius Caesar lay dying in Rome, America is being systematically killed by those who have acted independently, yet collectively, while concealing their maliciousness behind a cloak of liberty.

If we do not stop it, when America takes her last breath of freedom and greatness, those who wielded the daggers will panic and flee in fear and disclaim any responsibility, and the America we know will be gone forever.

History records that in the battle of Munda, Julius Caesar is quoted as saying, "In the past I have fought for victory, but today I fight for my life." Those of us who love America have fought and won many victories for our nation, but now we as America's majority must stand and fight for her life.

Slander, criticism, hurt, doubt, intimidation, and fear must never stop us. It is in essence a deadly game of chicken. Who will give way first? It cannot be we who do so, because the results will be

permanent.

The Call to Be Bold

I n July of 2003, Reverend Joe Wright was invited to pray for the opening session of the Kansas Senate. Little did anyone know what was in store. This was not going to be the usual canned prayer of a politically correct minister.

Reverend Wright would deliver a prayer of passion and conviction from deep within the soul, a prayer that would expose how some in America have committed the unthinkable and justified it in terms acceptable to a deceived society. Here is what he said:

> Heavenly Father, we come before you today to ask your forgiveness and to seek your direction and guidance. We know your Word says, "Woe to those who call evil good," but that is exactly what we have done.

We have lost our spiritual equilibrium and reversed our values. We confess that we have ridiculed the absolute truth of Scripture and called it pluralism.

We have exploited the poor and called it the lottery. We have rewarded laziness and called it welfare. We have killed our unborn and called it choice. We have shot abortionists and called it justifiable. We have neglected to discipline our children and called it building self-esteem. We have polluted the air with profanity and pornography and called it freedom of expression. We have ridiculed the time-honored values of our forefathers and called it enlightenment.

Search us, O God, and know our hearts today; cleanse us from every sin and set us free. Guide and bless these men and women who have been sent to direct us to the center of Your will and to openly ask these things in the name of Your Son, the living Savior, Jesus Christ. Amen!

Reverend Wright stood that day, boldly and without apology. He proclaimed the truth, disdaining how it may have been taken or accepted by the hearers. That prayer resonated with millions of people. Reverend Wright's church, Central Christian, received over six thousand phone calls. All but forty-seven were positive, proving that the majority of Americans feel strongly about the assault on truth.

These times that we live in call for boldness from those of us who have seethed but said nothing. We must be bold to expose lies and to present the unvarnished truth without regard for what the fallout might be from the radical minority in America.

Most people who hold responsible positions in government, media, education, and religion have chosen to shirk the responsibility they have to the American people. These men and women, who by virtue of their coveted positions in public life, are depended on to guard America's values: to expose corruption, evil, and wrong, no matter how it comes packaged.

But, alas, cowardice has overtaken too many, causing them to give in to political correctness and popularity, rather than seizing the opportunity to be bold and liberate imprisoned thinking with truth.

In writing this book, I knew that I must be bold and say what the majority of America is thinking but just will not say. Those of us who still hold truth in high esteem cannot be intimidated and give up our right to stem the tide of the unconscionable thinking that has America awash in philosophies whose end will be the destruction of our nation.

I love America and all that she has offered to my family and me. I am grateful for those who have given their lives to preserve her freedom and to those who are currently giving their lives to fight a new and deadly enemy.

I am resolved to remain silent no longer and to do what I can as an American to defend my country, without a hatred of people but with a fervent desire to meet wrong and untruth head-on and to do so with all the boldness that God gives me. Nathan Hale, the Revolutionary War patriot, said it best, "I can't do everything, but I can do something. What I can do, I ought to do; and what I ought to do, by the grace of God, I will do."

Chapter 1

Removing the Cloaks

—∽—

I have discovered in my experience that the light of public opinion shining brightly on the activities of any person or organization can do more to expose the true intent and purpose behind those activities than anything else can.

Those who attempt to cloak themselves in clever bywords, catch phrases, and emotional-sounding purposes are suddenly thrust into the searching and revealing light of public scrutiny and examination. The result is the majority of Americans have the opportunity to view them without the cloaks of choice and can make informed judgments based on truth, not on outward cloaks that are carefully constructed to conceal who they are and what kind of detrimental effects their activities are having on America. Public scrutiny has the awesome power to effect change and prevent the initial advance of maliciousness before it ever begins.

Make no mistake; being uneducated about what is happening in America will lead to the shock of discovering that the nation we love and cherish no longer exists. The values and rights that men and women died to ensure and that we hold in sacred trust will suddenly be gone forever.

For too long now, we as Americans have adopted a peace-at-any price philosophy. Those who would kill our nation have been able to level an all-out, unprincipled assault on reason, freedom, our heritage, proven social structure, order, and decency, incessantly tearing away the fabric that has made us so strong and secure in our personal lives, family lives, church lives, political lives, and America's overall life as a vibrant nation.

Our survival has always been dependent upon a discerning spirit and being able to distinguish right from wrong and good from evil. Over the last twelve years, we have made choices in American life that clearly demonstrate our discernment has been dimmed by the fraud of malice cloaked in liberty.

Why? Because wrong and evil have taken a very subtle and different approach in order to make themselves less distinguishable.

The new tactic of choice is "cloaking." In other words, it's covering what you really are all about and cleverly concealing what your true intents and purposes are, disguising what you are really up to, hiding the daggers under a cloak that people will find acceptable.

I can assure you, when we remove the cloak, it's not a pretty sight. Upon closer examination, it is easy to discover that what is being hidden is certainly not what is best for you and me and America. Instead, it's somebody's twisted idea of how things should be in order to further the cause of those energized by moral madness.

Self-serving has transcended into causes that will kill America if allowed to continue unchecked and unchallenged.

It is imperative for our society's continued existence that the truth be revealed, no matter the price we have to pay. Those social engineers of public chaos are counting on us to not go there, that is, to dare challenge sincerity and motives. If we do, we are labeled as right-wing bomb throwers, bigots, and hate-mongers. It's not about right-wing anything—it's about *right, period!*

I do not believe in hurling bombs at America's internal problems. Bombs blow up everything without regard for anybody. But I do believe we are compelled to confront these issues with surgeon-like precision and cut out the growth of anarchy.

I have talked to people from all walks of life in different states and towns. I know for a fact that the majority of Americans are frustrated, sickened, and very angry that the raucous voices of a rabid and fractured minority are continuing to dictate and force upon America ideologies that will guarantee our death as a nation.

What makes it even more disturbing is that people are confused by all the rhetoric that those individuals and organizations are using to persuade the public that their cause is a noble one, when in reality they are advancing maliciousness while cloaking it in liberty.

You can readily see the reasons why it is imperative that the cloaks be ripped away, and when they are, people will be shocked at what is revealed.

Confronted only by a few who sound the alarm, these individuals and groups have thus far gotten a virtually free ride and an unopposed fight. It is my personal conviction that the cultural war in

America is just about to begin, because the majority of Americans are ready to enter the fight.

I am an eternal optimist, not a doomsayer; but I fear, and with good cause, that if we cannot win this war with words of reason, then in the next decade frustrations will boil over into the streets of America.

Chapter 2

Assault on Our Culture

Cloaked as Entertainment and Progressive Thinking

—⁓—

Michael Moore is the newly anointed Hollywood attack dog, America's version of Joseph Goebbels, a propagandist bloated with an insidious hatred of America, foaming at the mouth with intellectual rabies and replete with venom for anything U.S.A. The adulation poured out on him by his fellow Americans and Bush-haters is nauseating, but at the same time somewhat mirthful in that the worship he is receiving is akin to the people who adored the emperor's new clothes. Remember the fairy tale? The emperor had no clothes, and the people applauded what they did not see.

Moore was crowned for a work of art, for his movie *Fahrenheit 9/11*. Did I say movie? I meant to say propaganda film, a mindless piece of trash that anybody with a video camera and a vendetta could film. I also find it interesting that Hezbollah wants to distribute this carefully cut and pasted lie to the Arab world. This is the guy who gently labels terrorist devils who cut off the heads of innocent people as "revolutionaries" and America as "a vile and intrusive enemy." From my vantage point, every time this pompous windbag opens his mouth, his tongue bayonets his brain.

Ironically, his movie title *Sicko* appropriately describes Moore himself. His latest box-office offering tells more lies than you will probably ever hear at one sitting.

The purpose of *Sicko* is to sell us on the idea of national health care. Wouldn't that be great—Congress deciding who needs medical care and who doesn't? If that doesn't frighten you, I frankly don't know what will.

For an example of failed national health care, look to Canada. The people there have reaped the bitter fruits of government medical care. Placing in the government's hands the right to play God and decide whether a person's quality of life or expected quantity of life meets the standard to qualify that person to be medically treated is simply asking for abuse. National health care would be especially devastating to the elderly, who might be termed ineligible for surgeries and procedures.

Is Michael Moore really concerned about people's health? Not a chance! He is yet another in a long line of self-serving "culture doctors" who use any means to feed their own egos and fatten their bank accounts. See him for what he really is. Moore is a tinsel-town con-man who has made a fortune off of America's capitalistic free enterprise while at the same time espousing the virtues of communist socialism. He has discovered sensitive issues that he knows will influence the passions of reasonable people and then he turns that emotional frenzy into financial gain.

Michael Moore has parlayed his assault on our culture into a multimillion dollar business. He travels the world, playing to audiences of glassy-eyed enemies of America. In Britain he said, "Americans are crappy people, the dumbest people on Earth," characterizing us as conniving, thieving, and smug. "Our stupidity is embarrassing, and we are totally uninformed on world issues." I guess he thinks his ignorant incivility is acceptable.

In Munich, Germany, he said, "Our brains are empty." He accused America of having "a reputation for creating sadness to the existence of foreign countries everywhere." I guess his brain is so soiled by secular indoctrinations that he forgot, if he ever knew, that America saved Britain's and France's hides—not to mention liberating Germany from a ruthless dictator who pitchforked women and children, or freeing the Iraqi people to look in mass graves for their loved ones who were slaughtered by Saddam Hussein.

Moore accuses us of being a nerve center of evil. Wow! That's pretty far-out, considering the ruthless, murderous regimes that exist today.

But, then, whoever said Michael Moore was in touch with reality or truth? After 9/11 he charged to every microphone he could find to blame that attack on past wars that we have been forced to fight in order to preserve freedom. He has railed to appreciative audiences in Germany (the world-class backstabbers) that America does not deserve the right to be heralded as the leader of the free world. I wonder who he thinks qualifies: France, the world-class coward, or North Korea's twisted little dictator?

These Hollywood types are waging an assault on our culture that is unprecedented in the history of this country. They attempt to portray those of us who seek to think rationally as idiots and buffoons, mocking anyone who has the audacity to oppose the culture they want to create.

Now get this! Think with me! These *would-be* rulers are attempting to do a rewrite of America's culture, yet their culture is one of multiple divorces (if they get married; most don't), designer drugs, murders, suicides, babies born out of wedlock, adultery, betrayal, fraud, and using human beings like rags and discarding them when they are no longer relevant, selling their souls and reputations to the highest bidder. They would re-create America's culture like their own: a culture of screaming, cursing radicals who envision an America patterned after their fantasy world of entertainment and far removed from the reality that the rest of America lives in every day, having been spoiled by fan worship and drunk with fame to the point that the high value they place on their opinions is a total fantasy.

The fact that these culture-war icons see themselves as qualified engineers of social change is absolutely appalling. They obviously have mistaken star status for all-knowing godhood.

This kind of logic is coming from people who make their living pretending. Did you get that? Pretending. I think one could safely say they have become so open-minded that their brains have fallen out. The assault Hollywood is carrying out on America's culture threatens to obliterate a long-existing culture that establishes boundaries of behavior where manners and mutual respect are prevalent. This sorry bunch loves to be heard preaching tolerance, but they sure as heck don't exhibit any.

How does America fight back? Hit Hollywood where it hurts; through their advertisers, hit their money pouches. Don't attend movies starring radical actors and actresses or produced by those who want to reorder our society to fit their dream world. After all, it should not be necessary to suppress a gag reflex in order to see a movie, simply because you abhor the actor's personal attacks on our culture and our country.

Mark Cuban's movie "redacted" shamelessly denigrates American troops who are fighting terrorism. Cuban crosses the line of human decency with this vile piece of trash. He is a disgrace to this nation and he insults every military person who has ever fought to defend freedom. Every person should protest against his movie. We must take a stand and support our troops.

Hollywood has declared a culture war on America. They have proved that by the steps they have taken to shock our sense of decency and morality. Their weapons are this mind-set: *anything goes in life, no matter how damaging it is to our ordered culture.* If Hollywood can think of it, it has to be right for everybody. America's majority must join the fight to resist.

Another assault on our culture is coming from an unlikely source; unlikely, that is, until you think about it seriously: PETA (People for the Ethical Treatment of Animals).

Now, I love animals. They have always been a part of my life, but animals are not humans. They have feelings, but not a soul. When our dog Pal died after thirteen years with us, my wife and I cried for two days. We loved that dog. My sons grew up with him. When they left for college, my wife sat in the backyard crying, and Pal licked her face and comforted her. I love animals. We have owned dozens of cats over thirty-seven years of marriage and had many horses.

PETA is not about loving animals; they cloak their actions in that disguise. The real agenda is to dehumanize people, to cheapen human life by comparing animals to humans; and in some cases, animals receive a higher status than humans do.

This organization is widely accepted in society as being cred-ible. They are funded by the rich and famous and attract workers from radical groups with an ax to grind and who embrace an unrealistic view of humans and animals.

In a sweeping comparison, they adopted the phrase *holocaust on your plate,* comparing the processing of chickens with the German horror of cremating millions of Jewish prisoners, thus sending a message that the lives of chickens are as valuable as the lives of human beings. Any right-thinking person would find that comparison repulsive.

The secular humanist propaganda machine has continuously sought to lessen the value of human life, placing human creation on the same level as that of animals and thus erasing the concept of a divine Creator. Society has too often embraced this dangerous philosophy, thus rendering humans as discardable. At one point in their sordid history, some of PETA's female members sat topless in cages placed strategically on various city streets, attempting to equate the caging of people with the caging of circus animals.

But it seems PETA has gone to even greater lengths. Michael Janofsky wrote in the *New York Times* on December 25, 2005, that "the FBI was urged to investigate PETA by David Martosko, director of research for the Center for Consumer Freedom, a group supported by the food and restaurant companies, which are, among others, persistent PETA critics." Martosko pointed to contributions made by PETA to people linked to groups that the FBI describes as domestic terrorist organizations. He said "the contributions included $1,500 to a press officer for the Earth Liberation Front, which has been linked to fires at construction sites, and $2,000 to a spokesman for the Animal Liberation Front, which authorities say has been behind attacks against animal research labs, as well as $70,000 to a member who was later convicted of arson." There was also that national gathering of activists in 2001 when Bruce Friedrich, a PETA official, said, "Blowing stuff up and smashing windows was an effective way to liberate laboratory animals."

Martosko insisted that "the FBI surveillance of PETA is justified." These are certainly dangerous people with an agenda that exalts animals and degrades humans."

Where does that type of thinking come from? Pagan cultures. In India cobras bite and kill hundreds of men, women, and children every year, but the cobra is sacred and must not be killed. In pagan cultures, cows are sacred. Wild cows roam in villages and walk into huts, goring adults and trampling little children. Many people are starving, yet they won't kill cows for food. Why is that? They place a higher value on animals than they do on human life.

That's insane! No rational person could embrace that type of thinking, but the members of PETA do. It's interesting that many of PETA's supporters are members of mystical religions. Well, well, what a coincidence!

In a culture where animals hold a higher status than humans, there is disease, death, immorality, and hopelessness. You see, when you place a greater value on anything other than human life, you cannot survive. You and I would risk our lives to save a stranger, but if we ran a high risk of dying in the process, we would most likely not risk it on an animal.

A human being is the zenith of God's creation. Were you aware that because of PETA's efforts and pressures on politically correct politicians, in some states a man can receive more jail time for killing an animal (though that's wrong) than for beating and raping a woman? Unbelievable, but true. Make no mistake; we cannot survive if thinking like that takes hold in our culture.

The effort to dehumanize people and humanize animals started with secular humanism, and PETA is carrying the torch. In western states, PETA has been instrumental, along with the kook fringe of the environmentalist movement, in relocating wolves, bears, and mountain lions. These animals, when removed from their original habitats, begin to range for food. They start killing young calves and sheep, causing ranchers to lose their livelihood. But PETA, supported by environmentalists, has persuaded the federal government to not allow ranchers to kill these growing packs of wolves. Furthermore—and this is the frightening part—mountain lions and bears are foraging into neighborhoods, dragging family pets and even small children out of yards and killing them.

Now, you would think there would be an outrage and the animals would not take precedence over the safety of humans, but you would be wrong. PETA presses the federal government to protect animals, even at great risk to people. If we allow ourselves to become a pagan nation, then we will surely suffer the consequences.

Have you stopped at a traffic light recently and had your ears assaulted by a dull, repetitive thud that shakes your car? Or have you been privileged to hear vulgar lyrics from somebody's radio playing a CD of some half-wit mouthing epithets and hurling profanity at women or discussing sex acts? Welcome to the new music culture:

punk rock and gangsta rap, led by such notable citizens as Ludacris, Jadakiss, Eminem, and Nas.

One of the most notorious of this group is Snoop Dogg (Calvin Broadus), who was arrested as he left NBC studios for investigation of illegally possessing a handgun and drugs. The rapper was taken into custody, along with two members of his entourage.

Broadus is a convicted felon under investigation for possessing a firearm, possessing cocaine, and transporting marijuana. He has been arrested several times since then. Dogg, as he calls himself, is one of the top-selling rappers in the country. No wonder our culture is deteriorating when a thug like this influences young minds with his blatant criminal behavior and music.

The rap group Three 6 Mafia won an Oscar for its sympathy-seeking hit "It's Hard Out Here for a Pimp." Not to be left out, Black Entertainment Television cashes in by routinely televising concerts and showcasing rap groups, the more ganglike the better. They provide a platform for those who depict gutter behavior that is shocking to the senses of young listeners and desensitizing them to the reality and consequences of violent behavior. The despicable practice of dogfighting is even being promoted in some gangsta rap lyrics.

This music glorifies nudity, violence, physical assault, alcohol and drug use, free sex, rape, and murder. The lyrics are rapidly eroding respect for other people, whipping many youth into a frenzy of violent behavior toward parents and one another, and making the streets of Anytown America an increasingly dangerous place to live.

This music has also been instrumental in redesigning fashion. Youth and young adults dress in clothes that bear a strong resemblance to rags, with holes, tears, and pockets dragging the ground! In the culture of years gone by, we were ashamed to have a hole in the knee of our clothing or to have our behinds hanging out. Now it's cute! No! It's uncultured and uncivilized. There are youth in our own nation, and certainly in other countries, who would be overjoyed to have a piece of clothing without tears or holes. However, here in the United States, it is the fashion of choice. Have we completely lost our minds?

Britney Spears, though not advocating violence but promoting nudity and stupidity, is one of the worst examples in America of how *not to dress*. She looks as if a deranged alien designed her clothes. The worst part is mothers who go into stores and buy this junk clothing for kids when they throw fits to dress weird.

If dress and music are reflective of culture, then, friend, we are in deep trouble. It is no wonder terrorists think we are an easy mark. We look like we are! It's not surprising that cults believe young people to be easy targets for their brainwashing. They think, *Just look at how extreme they dress, and surely their thinking will be just as extreme. They will entertain any idea or fad.* Today negative role models act immature and goofy, flaunt their moral shallowness, and try to escape the consequences of breaking the law. Paris Hilton is a prime example.

The pagan practice of body piercing is pushing our culture to the limits. Now, you know, I'm not talking about ladies' pierced earrings. I'm talking about piercing noses, tongues, eyebrows, lips, and other unmentionables. Some people look as though they have been attacked by a staple gun. Medical doctors say these piercings, more often than not, result in infections; and in some severe cases, the infections lead to death.

Many young people who resemble a person in *National Geographic* can't get a job. They become depressed and commit crimes. Then, as usual, society is blamed. But all they need to do is look in the mirror. You see, they don't understand. If you ignore the mores of society, you do so at your own detriment.

It is crystal clear. That which is passing as a new culture is having a chilling effect on America. We can no longer accept the fact that our culture of refinement and boundaries will always be a part of American life.

A civilized society is set apart by its culture or lack thereof. Syndicated columnist Thomas Sowell said, "There is a culture war going on within the United States—and in fact within Western civilization as a whole—which may ultimately have as much to do with our survival or failure to survive as the war on terrorism." Mr. Sowell is right on target with that statement.

We must be quick to recognize the assault on our culture cloaked as entertainment and progressive thinking. The majority of Americans must enlist in the war against our culture, lest we live to see America become a pagan nation and a culture without a conscience.

Chapter 3

Social Indoctrination

Cloaked as Public Education

—◊—

The term *public education* is a misnomer in our modern society. The public long ago lost its influence on public education.

I graduated from public school, as my sons did, so I am not anti-public school, but facts are facts. What was public school even ten years ago is not public school today. What passes for public education is not even remotely what it was intended to be.

The biggest problem is how it has changed in nature and scope. Formerly the word *public* meant the school was for the public to educate their children. It was staffed by public servants and funded by public dollars. The general public had a major influence in its structure, discipline, and overall function. The role of parents in public education was significant.

But today the public has been replaced, at least in principle if not in name, by the word *government*. Parents are no longer able to influence their children's education as they did in the past. Parent-teacher organizations are now confined to baking cookies, holding bazaars, and having rummage sales.

Even the national PTA can no longer be trusted because of its liberal political and social agendas. If you check them out, they are about 85 percent opposed to what most parents want for their children in school. Over the past twenty years, I have taken note of the steady turn to the left by the PTA. They are no longer an advocate for parents and students, but instead are pursuing an educationally dangerous agenda.

I would encourage parents to leave this radical organization so they won't be used to promote that which will undermine what is important. Join the local PTO where parents can elect to pay dues and where funds raised remain locally to achieve goals and not forced educational subterfuge.

These out-of-touch organizations need to receive a message loud and clear from every concerned American.

Their message is unmistakable: *we want your child, your money, your labor, but don't tell us how to run the school.* The government will do that through the ACLU and the National Education Association. If parents object to sex education that espouses the philosophy "Everybody is going to do it, so use protection." If parents object to loose rules or complain about a lack of rules, they are viewed as parental troublemakers who are just ignorant of new age education.

I have personally talked to school board members who have spent $25,000 to win an expensive popularity contest. Most are unqualified to make decisions on something as important as educating our future leaders.

Most teachers and principals are members of the National Education Association, a radical political policy organization guised as a teachers' union. The NEA's founding function was to develop ways to better train teachers and lobby for better funding, pay, benefits, and retirement. It was supposed to fulfill the mission statement and not become partisan in any way.

The present NEA is currently spending hundreds of thousands of dollars to elect Democrats who will be sympathetic in helping them liberalize education. This has made public schools a hotbed for social indoctrination. America's schoolchildren are used as guinea pigs for social experimentation and with disastrous results. Certain psychologists are encouraged to come to parent-teacher organization meetings and discuss child-behavior patterns. If you observe and listen carefully, you will notice almost every negative trait that is discussed is inherent to some degree in all children. When the meeting ends, gullible parents rush to the speaker asking for his or her card, distraught that little Timmy or little Susie has one of these symptoms of abnormal behavior.

Dr. John Rosemond, a leading and respected child psychologist, has written numerous articles on the drugging of America's children. Ritalin seems to be the corrective method of choice to stem behavior that most times is normal and requires parental time, love, and discipline—not drugs! That's a parental cop-out. It is simply wrong to convince parents that a normal child's behavior is somehow antisocial and could be a deep, dark personality disorder.

It should be difficult enough to tell parents of a correct diagnosis for a child with behavioral problems, much less telling parents with a normal child that their child is abnormal. That's reckless! The NEA continues to encourage teachers to advocate and parents to accept this irresponsible type of thinking. Why? Because then teachers don't have to deal with the rambunctious child. The child is too doped up to be a problem. That is certainly not the way to train a child to adapt to his or her surroundings and to learn social interaction with other children. Children who are too quickly diagnosed and put on calming drugs are victims of socially indoctrinated adults.

In his journal, *Health & Healing,* Dr. Julian Whitaker writes: "Actresses Kirstie Alley and Kelly Preston and others testified before the Florida legislative in support of a bill that would end the despicable practice of forcing Florida's children to take drugs in order to attend public schools. Parents can be told that their child must take Ritalin or some other psychotropic drug or they cannot attend school. If the parents disagree, child protection services may place the child in a foster home so he can be drugged by the state in order to continue his education." Dr. Whitaker was supporting a bill that would stop this insane practice.

Dr. Whitaker further writes, "This kind of thing could never have happened forty years ago. Similar to today, some kids were more active than others, some learned more slowly, but all received a high-quality education." He says, "I don't remember a single student ever taking psychotropic drugs, much less receiving them as a prerequisite for attending school."

Dr. Whitaker further states: "Kids are no different today, but our public schools are different. They are flush with child psychologists and brainwashed teachers who feel that 'behavioral patterns' are more important than academics. Consequently, the education delivered by many public schools stinks." Dr. Whitaker continues that "test results show that a whopping two-thirds of middle and high school students cannot read proficiently. SAT scores have dropped so dramatically that the test had to be *dumbed down*."

Face it; public high schools choked with psychobabble graduate millions of short-tempered bubbleheads who don't know anything and can't do anything. Dr. Whitaker says, "Today public schools have become psychiatric wards, complete with 'mental health' personnel seemingly intent on drugging as many kids as possible." Academics have taken a back seat to the perverted view that "self-esteem is engendered by removing the stresses of actually having to learn something."

This does not increase self-esteem; it destroys it. Self-esteem stems from accomplishment. Eliminate the measurements of academic-success tests and grades and you eliminate any possibility of self-esteem.

Dr. Whitaker further adds an astonishing statistic: "Today, close to nine million school children are taking these drugs. That is almost one in five students in America. At the rate we're going, 80 percent of schoolchildren will be taking psychotropic drugs within the next ten years." Dr. Whitaker writes that "Kirstie Alley poignantly and dramatically revealed the tragic side of child-drugging by showing pictures of smiling children now dead from suicide or confirmed drug reactions."

In this article, Dr. Whitaker also quotes Dr. Fred Baughman Jr., a neurologist from San Diego, that "there are no blood tests, X-rays, scans or other screening tools that can be used to support a diagnosis of ADD, ADHD, or any other psychiatric 'disease.'" It's all a fraud.

Fortunately for America's schoolchildren, Dr. Whitaker states that the Citizens Commission on Human Rights has been waging war against psychiatric abuse on human rights since 1969. This dedicated group was instrumental in the passage of a federal law that prohibits school districts from requiring children to take psychotropic drugs as a condition for attending school.

However, state law can override federal law in some cases. I am thankful for Dr. Whitaker and those who are fighting for children. We must be diligent.

In another incident, the San Francisco Board of Education voted to ban Junior ROTC in the city's high schools. This affected more than sixteen hundred students. On what premise was this insane act predicated? That the U.S. military is awful and should not be glorified or admonished.

Bill O'Reilly coined the phrase *San Francisco values,* and he is right.

Nancy Pelosi, the new speaker of the House, and her loopy constituents have embraced a set of values that are stunning and destructive to society and public education.

I talked to a number of parents who have boys, and they told me that their sons pay a price in school just for being boys. I looked at a class picture that well illustrates my point. The girls were hamming it up for the camera and the female teacher was joining in, but the boys were standing back, no smiles and looking subdued. This teacher has declared war on the boys in her class.

Here's the knee-jerk theory. If a little boy pulls a little girl's pigtail on the playground, then he has the potential for domestic violence. The NEA and many schools want to discourage recess because boys wrestle and tackle each other, play war games, and play-fight. They say that is allowing them to develop aggressive tendencies. What garbage! What is a boy to do when he is a grown man and confronted by a bully? Tell his wife, "Honey, you handle it"?

This brings me to my next issue in public education, and that is "erasing gender." In other words, kids should be ashamed to be specifically male or female. They should not possess traits of a specific gender, but it's fine to be homosexual. There should never be any distinction made in dress, mannerisms, likes, or dislikes. They are just children, and boys are encouraged to be feminine while girls are encouraged to be masculine.

Public schools are losing their identity. An article in Agape Press tells of an account in Pennsylvania of East Brook Elementary teacher Heather Kramer reading her students the book *King and King*, a story about a prince who spurns a number of eligible princesses in order to marry another prince. The story ends with two men marrying and sharing a kiss. When parents Rob and Robin Wirthlin complained about what took place, the school's principal told them that no parental notification was required nor would it be given before future discussions on homosexual "marriage." I hope those parents pinned a civil lawsuit to that principal's forehead.

On a website posting, [2007 WorldNetDailey.com] "Mom and Dad" as well as "husband and wife" effectively have been banned from California schools under a bill signed by Governor Arnold Schwarzenegger, who with his signature also ordered public schools to allow boys to use girls restrooms and locker rooms, and vice versa, if they choose.

"We are shocked and appalled that the governor has blatantly attacked traditional family values in California," said Karen England, executive director of Capitol Resource Institute. "With this decision, Governor Schwarzenegger has told parents that their values are irrelevant. Many parents will have no choice but to pull their children out of the public schools that have now become sexualized indoctrination centers,." "Arnold Schwarzenegger has delivered young children into the hands of those who will introduce them to alternative sexual lifestyles," said Randy Thomasson, president of Campaign for Children and Families, which worked to defeat the plans. "This means children as young as five years old will be mentally molested in school classrooms. Shame on Schwarzenegger and the Democrat politicians for ensuring that every California school becomes a homosexual-bisexual-transsexual indoctrination center," he said.

The Gay, Lesbian, and Straight Education Network (GLSEN) has long advocated school curriculum that promotes children cross-dressing. A homosexual group at the Buena Vista Elementary School in San Francisco created this program.

Concerned Women for America exposed a GLSEN-run sex education program in the state of Massachusetts that was, in essence, pure pornography, revealing that homosexual instructions had inflicted graphic depictions of revolting and physically harmful sex acts on children as young as fourteen. This has no place in public education, and America better become incensed at the liberties taken by those they entrust their children to.

Parents need to also be warned about Judith Levine's book *Harmful to Minors: The Perils of Protecting Children from Sex*. This piece of trash from the mind of an idiot has found its way into some public schools. Levine says, "Sex is not harmful to children. . . . There are many ways even the smallest children can participate." Her book is peppered with quotations from perverted pedophiles who want to legalize sex between adults and children. Wake up, America!

Kids' minds today are already on overload from too much information too soon without public education literally burning their minds up. We must understand that the only chance children have at a healthy emotional life is for moral, thinking adults to protect them from sexual deviants who would destroy their lives.

Some black children are poked fun at for being too white, white children are accused of not being black enough, and Hispanics are called nobodys. Because that is allowed in public education, there is an identity crisis. Parents have had it with schools promoting ideologies and social experiments that they are diametrically opposed to. The public is being forced to submit their children to the gay agenda, Islam, and a list of other issues that have absolutely nothing to do with education.

Then there is the dumbing down of education. It is justified this way: if you give the grades earned and they are bad, you damage the self-esteem of that student. That is so much baloney! How will a kid ever get ahead in life by being rewarded for nonachievement? That's absurd! But the thinking is, lower the curriculum in order that the most uneducated can get it. Put it on a lower shelf.

Why would a school district do that? Higher test scores bring in more money to the districts. Incompetent principals receive awards, and everybody goes home happy. There's one *major* problem: it's dishonest! The parents and administrators who favor dumbing down education also play down scholars programs for high achievers. Honors classes have all but disappeared in some schools.

I read a newspaper account about a principal who changed grades of minority students so they could graduate from high school. Now keep in mind, they failed the course study. The teachers saw them graduating and reported the principal to the school board. He was fired, right? No! He was transferred to another school.

That kind of behavior goes hand in hand with hiring totally unqualified teachers in order to fill quotas. It's the students who ultimately suffer the consequences, because they are not being properly taught.

Parents have a right to expect their children to be educated by qualified and honest educators. They have the right to expect their children to learn the subjects that are required, but not to be indoctrinated with philosophies that are contrary to their own. Parents should expect schools to consistently do the job they are taxpayer-supported to do, and that's to educate.

The pet project of liberal education is radical sex education, which actually promotes free sex among teens and derides abstinence education. Statistics prove that "Just don't do it" is the only way to ensure against teen pregnancy and venereal disease. I was told about one teacher who went so far as to tell her class that oral sex was not sex. I guess she is a disciple of Bill Clinton.

It is dangerously irresponsible to toy with the minds of young people when the consequences are so devastating and life-altering. It is intellectually dishonest to be derelict to the call of educating children in the subjects that prepare them for life in favor of social indoctrination, constantly broaching subject matter that should be off-limits to schools. Which do you think is more important: teaching a student how to have sex or how to read?

The misguided so-called sex education programs in public schools actually encourage students to have sex rather than teach responsibility to one's body and future. Teachers thinly disguise the programs' intents by briefly mentioning abstinence as an after-thought while openly promoting promiscuity.

My premise is this: if you are going to teach anything to a student in a public school, then do it honestly, *not* from your socially progressive viewpoint because the fallout from early sexual activity in teens can be seen in so many ruined lives. There is no place in public education for reckless instruction on *any* subject.

Is it reckless? You be the judge. The Christian Law Association's legal agent says:

> Forty- two percent of boys and thirty-three percent of girls between fifteen and seventeen have had intercourse. An estimated 80 percent of 15-year-old girls will have a baby before age twenty. Eighty-five percent of the one million teen pregnancies each year in the United States are unplanned.
>
> Nineteen million teens are infected with sexually transmitted diseases *every* year in America. Compare these STD numbers with statistics from previous generations. In the 1960s at the start of America's "sexual revo-

lution," 1 out of every 32 students was infected with an STD. By 1983 that number had jumped to 1 in 18, and by 1996 the number was 1 in 4. Sexually active girls are nearly three times more likely to attempt suicide than girls who are not sexually active, and sexually active boys are eight times more likely to attempt suicide than other boys who are not sexually active.

Do you think public school sex education is working? I certainly don't, and the facts prove it.

Now, there are many fine and dedicated public school teachers who take seriously their call to impart learning to others. But there should be no place in education for those who see their position as a soapbox to indoctrinate students with their brand of liberalism, doing such things as distorting history, teaching the Holocaust as myth, and making God irrelevant.

In a number of our public schools, the dishonesty of curriculum is appalling. Traditional, core-subject teaching has been abandoned in favor of left-wing liberal social causes that the teachers hope will indoctrinate students to pursue social activism. Students educated in this manner will be seriously shortchanged in their pursuit of higher academic achievements.

Furthermore, America is systematically portrayed as selfish, unkind, and as a bully nation. We are no longer the standard for free enterprise, capitalism, liberty, and freedom. Students are being taught that they should be ashamed to be Americans, that America is fraught with insurmountable problems unless social causes drive the engine.

Such teaching will produce a generation of adults that sees America as not worth defending from a foreign enemy because the principles that have made us so strong in the past are faulty. These social-activist educators are destroying the future of these students and the country they hope to pursue happiness in.

I remember one college professor who said he could not wait each year for the freshmen to attend his class so that he could destroy their faith. Christianity was his central choice. This is the kind of behavior we can expect from institutions that use such books as *A Godless Constitution*. Something has gone terribly awry in public education when students who attend a college or university to better themselves academically have to wade through a morass of liberal bias and radical opinion just to glean enough from the course study in order to graduate with a command of the subject.

Fox News reported that Kevin Barrett, a Wisconsin professor, is telling his students that the 9/11 attack and subsequent disaster was an *inside job*. He railed that it was carried out by our own government. It should frighten us that such a head case has the attention of impressionable young minds.

The most compelling case for the deterioration of public schools is the lack of structured discipline. I find it interesting that when godly principles were taught in school, along with respect and enforced discipline, our schools were so different from how they are today. God has been removed, for all practical purposes, and the *dangerous* Ten Commandments are gone.

Schools and politicians fall all over themselves to try to educate juvenile criminals. They spend thousands of dollars trying to keep these types of teenagers in school. They actually do forums on how to entice drug-using, drug-dealing, gun-toting, and gang-running thugs in school. Why the devil would you want to? Let them go. They only make schools dangerous for students who are there to learn.

So is public education better? Well, just ask the resource officers assigned to public schools (these are police officers who work in public schools to stop violence and the flow of drugs). They will quickly tell you that they would rather be raiding a crack house than endure the attitudes and filthy language of literally half the students. Why do they feel this way? No discipline!

The root cause of such disrespect is parental intimidation and parents who defend their thugs. Especially vocal are some black parents. The problem is the state of those particular families. They don't rear their children to succeed. They are given all the reasons they can't succeed. Years ago most black families took great pride in their children, but today they see them as liabilities.

Some white parents are guilty of defending their skinheads, and wealthy parents cover up the sins of their children. They buy their way out of crime by calling in political favors for quick fixes. I distinctly remember one family court judge asking a seventeen-year-old why he was vandalizing cars in a wealthy neighborhood. The boy answered, "I got with the wrong crowd." The steely-eyed judge said, "No, you are the wrong crowd."

Then there are threats by the ACLU, the NAACP, and the Rainbow/Push Coalition. What is the end result of all this? We are hosting gangs, drugs, assaults, rapes, guns, and knives in public schools.

One in twenty students has intentionally skipped school to avoid being attacked.[Fox News] This outrage could be and should be stopped, but school boards cater to threats. Teachers have told me that school administrators almost always side with angry, unreasonable parents and their children when conflicts arise. Unless, of course, it is a parent who objects to classroom time being wasted on inappropriate subject matter or demands that other students not be allowed to disturb the class, thus preventing good students from hearing instructions. That particular parent is ignored while the irresponsible parent is catered to.

I think the phone message that the staff at a high school in California devised is indicative of problematic parents. The staff voted unanimously to record it for the public. This was the answer to parental backlash because the school implemented a policy that required both students and parents to accept sole responsibility for their children's absences and missing homework assignments. Now, that should not be too much to ask of caring parents who are involved in both their child's education and life in general.

Some of the erring parents were suing teachers because they wanted their children's failing grades changed to passing grades, even though the students had been absent fifteen to thirty times during one semester of the school year. These students, mind you, did not even attempt to complete enough academic requirements to pass the coursework.

Here is the message the staff recorded:

> Hello! You have reached the automated answering service of your school. In order to assist you in connecting to the appropriate staff person, please listen to all of your options before making a selection.

> 1. To lie about why your child is absent, press one.
> 2. To make excuses for why your child did not do his or her homework, press two.
> 3. To complain about what we do, press three.
> 4. To swear at staff members, press four.

5. To ask why you did not get information that was already enclosed in your newsletter and in several flyers mailed to you, press five.

6. If you want us to raise your child, press six.

7. If you want to reach out and touch, slap, or hit someone, press seven.

8. To request for the third time this year that your child have a different teacher, press eight.

9. To complain about bus transportation, press nine.

10. To complain about school lunches, press zero.

11. If you realize that this is the real world and your child must be accountable and responsible for his/her own behavior, classwork, homework, and it's not the teacher's fault for your child's lack of effort, then hang up and have a nice day.

I am certain there are many good schools across America that would love to implement that message to parents. Irresponsible parents just don't seem to get it. They are ruining their kids!

I read the following recently, and I thought was excellent. It defines the mammoth task that dedicated teachers must face. The author is unknown.

After being interviewed by the school administration, the eager teaching prospect said, "Let me see if I've got this right. You want me to go into that room with all those kids and fill their every waking moment with a love for learning, and I'm supposed to instill a sense of pride in their ethnicity, modify their disruptive behavior, observe them for signs of abuse, and even censor their T-shirt messages and dress habits.

"You want me to wage a war on drugs and sexually transmitted diseases, check their backpacks for weapons of mass destruction, and raise their self-esteem. You want me to teach them patriotism, good citizenship, sportsman-ship, fair play, how to register to vote, how to balance a checkbook, and how to apply for a job.

"I am to check their heads for lice, maintain a safe environment, recognize signs of antisocial behavior, and make sure all students pass the state exams, even those who don't come to school regularly or complete any of their assignments.

"Plus, I am to make sure that all the students with handicaps get an equal education regardless of the extent of their mental or physical handicaps. I am to communicate regularly with the parent by letter, telephone, newsletter, and report card.

"All of this I am to do with just a piece of chalk, a computer, a few books, a bulletin board, a big smile *and* on a starting salary that qualifies my family for food stamps. You want me to do all of this, and then you tell me *I can't pray?*"

When the impact of these thoughts hits home with America, we can truly sympathize with *good* public education teachers and support them.

A new study by the nonpartisan Public Agenda found that nearly eight in ten teachers (78 percent) said unruly students are quick to remind them that they have rights or their parents can sue.

Nearly half of the teachers surveyed (49 percent) reported that they have been accused of unfairly disciplining a student by simply demanding order in the classroom. More than half the teachers (55 percent) said that when districts back down from parents or left-leaning pressure organizations, it causes major discipline problems in our nation's schools.

More than one in three teachers has left public education for fear of violence. High school sports at one time was an extracurricular activity for students who made qualifying grades and maintained a level of acceptable behavior. That day, too, has passed away. There is virtually no minimum grade requirement at present. Principals will lie and say there is but know full well that athletes curry academic favors.

Why is that allowed? Two reasons: to win games and to avoid discriminating against a student athlete who has chosen to remain academically ignorant. After all, sports may be his or her ticket to a life of luxury. Too often we see a news report about a local athlete who has been arrested for assault, theft, or gang activity. Yet when game night arrives, this thug is on the field to play. Many of these Friday-night criminal athletes go on to universities to rape, burglarize, and, in some cases, to commit murder.

How can this happen? The athlete has no character, and the school has no discipline policy. Too many coaches no longer make being a good citizen a requirement to participate in sports.

I began this chapter by talking about the metamorphosis of public schools from public to government. The biggest obstacle we as Americans face in the battle to make public education accountable is the cold, hard fact that it is no longer guided by a caring and concerned public, but by an interfering, bureaucratic government. Unfortunately, misguided government is ruling public education and killing America's intellectual future in the process.

Abraham Lincoln said, "The philosophy in the classroom in one generation will be the philosophy of the government in the next." Just one generation bottle-fed on social indoctrination, and the next generation we lose a nation.

If our schools are to have a chance, then we must be active participants and not be stymied or deterred from our right to make a positive impact. If we are passive, then indoctrination cleverly cloaked as education will cause America to reap a bitter harvest.

Chapter 4

Race-Baiters

Cloaked in Civil Rights

—ɯ—

Racial discrimination is a statement that evokes emotions that run the gamut from resentment by people who are discriminated against legitimately to burning anger from people who have experienced the abuses of racial discrimination charges.

Now, every United States citizen understands that there are federal laws to protect any person from racial discrimination. So begs the question, Do African Americans need the NAACP? I submit that they don't.

Why? For starters, the NAACP represents only about 20 percent of the total African American population in the United States. The percentage is low for obvious reasons. The NAACP has lost its credibility as a viable organization. Most African Americans distance themselves from its radical agenda. They have chosen instead to work and live in harmony and use the laws on the books that protect us all if we need them.

The NAACP is not the only way to communicate with African Americans. The African American Leadership Council, I understand, is doing a good job. There are a number of very credible and conservative voices for blacks in America.

But, of course, Kweisi Mfume calls them ventriloquist dummies, voices of their puppet masters. The NAACP is parroting Democrats and MoveOn.org. Credible African Americans don't want to be identified with an organization whose national board chairman, Julian Bond, rants and raves, calling conservatives in America "the Taliban" and further refers to them as the "white people's party" and "a crazed swarm of right-wing locusts." (By the way, fanatical Muslims use the term *crazed swarm of locusts* frequently.) Bond polarizes the race debate and sets up blacks as all things Democrat. He recklessly accused President Bush of planning to repeal the Fourth Amendment of the Constitution, which guarantees equal protection under the law.

The NAACP takes advantage of the guilt trip they have laid on America to the point that now reverse discrimination has reared its ugly head. To the NAACP, it's not just about rights any longer. It's about special rights, fomenting the concept of reparations, along with the National Reparations Committee. Their goal is to influence liberal politicians to pass a law that would allow deducting a certain amount of money from the paycheck of every white American to pay for the injustices of slavery then dispensing those monies to every African American that buys into racial extortion.

If you say that is preposterous, then you would be right! But that is what Omowale Clay of the National Millions (more like hundreds) Reparation Committee wants: to have white America pay her and every one of her (seeking free money) followers for slavery, as they chant, "You stole us, you sold us, you owe us."

Well, I've got news for Ms. Clay! Neither I nor any other white American living today has stolen or sold blacks for slavery, and we sure as the devil don't owe her anything. If Ms. Clay or her followers have been stolen or sold, then I say call the FBI. Don't try to inject yourself into past history.

The proponents of this completely ridiculous request claim they want forty acres and a mule. Well, this is laughable! When I was a boy, my grandfather let me plow with a mule a few times, and it's hard work. So I can assure you, this particular crowd does not want a mule, because they would have to work rather than try to lay a guilt trip on white America and invent yet one more way to extract money they haven't earned. I have carefully observed people who want the ridiculous. They won't mow their lawns, much less take care of forty acres.

Don't you find it interesting that they don't accuse the ancestors of African tribal chiefs of slavery? They are the ones who captured and sold slaves to slave traders! But, no! It's whites living today who they believe should pay for the sins of men who lived two hundred years ago.

Well, fortunately, there are millions of people, African Americans among them, who find this absurd claim to be both offensive and divisive. How dare Ms. Clay accuse me and millions of other white Americans of being slave owners! I resent that for many reasons.

One of which is that I was reared on a farm by my grandparents. My grandfather was a sharecropper and lived crop to crop. An

African American family lived nearby. They had nine children. Every fall my grandfather gave the family pork, beef, and home-canned vegetables to sustain them through the winter. My grandmother churned and gave them milk and butter for the children. The father of that family occasionally helped my grandfather on his farm. My grandfather could not afford help, but he paid him anyway because he knew the man had no other work and ten mouths to feed.

My grandfather drove a wagon to the sawmill and collected culled lumber to keep their house fixed up enough to be livable. My grandfather hauled corn ten miles to a grist mill to have it ground. He always had extra bags ground for this family so they could make bread. My grandmother sewed clothes for the children from scraps of cloth that she collected.

The mother of the family became seriously ill, and for two weeks my grandmother, using every home remedy available to her, nursed this woman back to health. Had she not helped her, she would have died.

Every month my grandmother invited them to our house, we enjoyed meals together, and I played with the children. We never saw one another as black or white, but just people who needed one another.

I want Ms. Clay, her followers, and the NAACP to understand that white America is fed up with being called racist every time a black organization like hers dreams up another way to get a free handout and further drive a wedge between black and white people. That's certainly not the type of dream Martin Luther King advocated. I don't owe Ms. Clay one dime, and neither does any other white American.

The Americans that I know, of every race, are working together, worshipping together, and striving to get along, treating one another with respect, while the NAACP thrives on division. But remember, it's the lifeblood of their existence, the means of their survival. The NAACP minions frequently utter the phrase *limited freedom*. That's a hoax! These members are as free as anybody in this nation. The NAACP limits their own freedom by abusing the gains that so many dedicated African Americans have made.

They constantly remind black Americans that they are in the minority, furthering the falsehood that they will be automatically treated unfairly by everybody else. This type of thinking stunts the personal growth of individuals and is a dream-killer.

The majority of Americans do not believe that being less in numbers guarantees victimhood. I have studied those who run to the NAACP screaming about rights, and most of them are not productive citizens who take pride in their own ability to succeed in life. They instead are looking for handouts they don't deserve, or they are trying to avoid being justly punished.

The reason others were successful is clear: they kept to their purpose with dignity and honor, and the cause of civil rights was respected.

When President Ronald Reagan died, one of the NAACP's state vice-president operatives, Reverend Joe Darby, accused President Reagan of supporting Osama bin Laden in Afghanistan, knowing full well that we were supporting the Afghan freedom fighters against Russia's unprovoked aggression. The mujahedeen were Afghan citizens, not Al-Qaeda. Osama bin Laden was a Saudi living in Saudi Arabia at the time. He did not come to Afghanistan until the Taliban came to power. These kinds of distortions are typical of the NAACP's religious operatives.

The NAACP labels anyone who opposes them as mean-spirited and divisive. Translated, that means anyone who won't cater to their whims. But you see, I can disagree without discriminating. They say that those of us who use the term *welfare queen* are bigots. All you have to do is stand in a grocery store line and observe a woman using food stamps to buy three carts full of groceries and wads of cash to buy beer, wine, and tobacco, and then watch as she drives away in a big new car. Hello! I just described a *welfare queen,* whether black or white.

The NAACP can yell loud and strong, but they don't do anything constructive to help black families. An unacceptable percentage of black children are born out of wedlock, and too many of black males between the ages of eighteen and thirty-five are involved in America's criminal justice system.

The NAACP has been notorious for sticking their noses into public schools and dumbing down education. They've been doing that since 1975. Why? Because they would rather lower the bar of academic achievement so slackers can graduate as opposed to making them earn a quality education that leads to being successful as others of all races do. When these goof-offs get a degree, it's virtually worthless. They protest businesses and the government for jobs, knowing they actually do not possess the education to do the job. If they are subsequently fired, they scream, Racism! This is also embarrassing to African Americans who have earned an education.

The majority of America is fed up with being called bigots just because they reject the racist agenda. That's what the NAACP is trying to impose on all Americans. Millions of people see right through their tactics. For example, every year at election time, the NAACP goes public with the same old lament: *conservatives are not willing to embrace their cause*. They claim a serious effort needs to be made to reach out to them.

Let's get real! NAACP members have sold their souls to the Democratic candidates by a nine to one margin, while the rest of black America elects candidates on merit. Let's face it; the NAACP stopped being a nonpartisan civil rights organization years ago when wild-eyed radicals began to lead them.

Julian Bond characterized the Republican Party as appealing to the underside of American culture, that group of Americans who reject democracy and equality, accusing Republicans of being dangerous and a constant threat to all civil rights, and wanting to bring back Jim Crow segregation. Yet when conservatives attempt to speak at one of their conventions, they are hooted down and not even extended the common courtesy one would accord a guest. They won't even consider the merits of any politician, black or white, who will not yield to every demand they make. The NAACP is not mainstream and fair, but radical left-wing bomb throwers who should not be accorded validity.

Republican candidates and conservative Democrats are put through the meat grinder. Distinguished and respected African Americans such as Colin Powell, Clarence Thomas, and Armstrong Williams are labeled "Uncle Toms." I guess these men just don't pass the NAACP's litmus test, but isn't it comforting to know that Jesse Jackson, Al Sharpton, and Julian Bond do?

Kweisi Mfume, the past leader of the NAACP, has partnered with the Democrats in order to pump new life into his sinking ship, and he knows that's true. He knows it's in their best interest to let radical join radical. There is no place else for them. It's not about civil rights; it's about politics, Democratic politics.

Have you noticed that the NAACP is on opposite ends of the spectrum from the majority of blacks in this country? Most blacks support the war against terror and are in favor of faith-based charity initiatives. They want school choice, but the NAACP's blind loyalty to the ultraliberal Democratic Party prevents them from representing all black Americans.

I have news for the NAACP; they are not representing people who make a clear distinction between those citizens who have the best interest of America at heart and those who are promoting a selfish agenda in order to line their collective pockets.

The NAACP is big on touting itself as working for the *common good* of all people, but surely not in present times. Daimler/Chrysler was planning to build a plant in South Carolina. The NAACP drove them out of the state. What was the earthshaking issue? The Confederate flag is a flag that people in South Carolina, black and white, ignore. When the company decided they would not consider South Carolina as a location to build a plant, many future jobs were lost that African Americans and others desperately needed. That certainly is not "common good."

The NAACP imposed a statewide boycott urging conventions and vacationers to stay away. Why? Was there a plague in South Carolina? No, it was the Confederate flag. Thankfully, the boycott was ignored. Even the black bikers came. But the boycott was very revealing in that the NAACP did not care that the majority of hotel and convention workers in South Carolina are African American. That proves, at least to me, that the NAACP does not have the best interest of all black people at heart.

Probably the most notorious race-baiter in America today is Jesse Jackson. His Rainbow/PUSH Coalition is all about money, lots of it. It's not about rights and not righting wrongs, and it's not about correcting discrimination practices, but about indiscriminately using race as an excuse to go into cities all over America and pummel people into submission with the dreaded word *racist*.

Make no mistake; when Jesse Jackson starts a battle with any organization or company, the first casualty in that battle is always truth. America needs to wake up and understand that Jesse Jackson's coalition is solely about injecting racism into every single incident that involves even one African American. Once the dreaded word *racist* is used, people become fearful and don't want to be branded as bigots in their communities. Following closely on fear comes the indignant cry for money. Jesse Jackson, unfortunately, has a long and murky history of inventing racism where there was never any intent of racism or none existed. He capitalizes on individuals who rush to disprove those charges by asking them for large donations.

Corporate America is a frequent target of Jesse Jackson's threats of baseless boycotts. What happens to America's consumers when the huge payoffs are made? You guessed it! Consumer prices go up to make up the deficit, and that is killing American consumerism.

I am puzzled at the corporate fear. Jesse Jackson and his supporters represent about 20 percent of the purchasing public. If everybody who supports Jackson stopped buying certain products, which they won't and we know it, it would not even be a blip on a corporation's financial radar. Corporations need to put a stop to it. The other 80 percent of consumers *will* buy their products and applaud them for not yielding to *corporate shakedowns*. Some of Jackson's donors are on the who's who list of American corporations.

Jesse Jackson is a legend in his own mind, and he wants to be a legend in ours. America should be outraged that he is afforded dignitary status by fawning, trembling politicians. We should be furious that our government allows him to go to other countries and schmooze with terrorists and interfere in sensitive issues that involve our national security. All the while, he's telling the world what a racist nation we are.

Why is it that nobody has called his hand on accepting large donations from suspect governments? I'll tell you why: it's because of the perceived power that he has. So what if he can get people who refuse to work to march down the street in the middle of the day? Does that make him somebody special? I say it does not.

It is clear that Jesse Jackson is an opportunist who uses race for his own personal advantage, and it feeds his massive ego. He is a master race-baiter with no shame.

What can I say about Al Sharpton and his National Action Network? He of Tawana Brawley fame! He who closes on an open microphone quicker than a linebacker closes on a running back. Al Sharpton said he and John Kerry would create ten million new jobs for African Americans. Who is he kidding? This guy lives in a fantasy world that is made worse by people who actually gave him money to run for president.

Al Sharpton sees every problem that blacks experience as caused by white people. I thought it was amazing that the Democratic Party would allow him to speak at their convention, knowing how he blames whites for too much rain or not enough.

Al Sharpton should listen to entertainer Bill Cosby's take on that issue, as reported in *The State News*, and I quote, "Too many black men are beating their wives while their children run around not knowing how to read or write." He chided blacks for wasting the prime opportunities that were given them through civil rights. He said, "The black community is attempting to hide its dirty laundry." He continued, "Let me tell you something—your dirty laundry gets out of school at two-thirty every day; it's cursing and calling each other n - - - - r in the streets. They think they are hip. They can't read, they can't write, they're laughing and going nowhere!"

He addressed a segment of black men this way, "You've got to stop beating up your women because you can't find a job, because you squandered your educational opportunity and now you're earning minimum wage." He said, "You cannot simply blame whites for problems such as teen pregnancy and high school dropout rates. We have to turn the mirror around. It's analgesic to talk about what the white man is doing against us, and it keeps a person frozen in their seat. It keeps you frozen in the hole you're sitting in!"

How courageous and honest Bill Cosby is! That's why America loves him. It is that type of character that has endeared him to decades of people. He is truly the kind of leader that African Americans desperately need.

We don't need people like the NAACP's minister Michael Muhammad, who on the O'Reilly Factor, admonished the nation that we were doing Michael Vick gross injustice by judging him. His assertion that Vick is singled out because he is a successful million-aire sports star is ridiculous! The federal grand jury had so much evidence presented to them, you could have filled a warehouse with it—not to mention the testimony of Vick's closest ally, who turned state's evidence. Minister Muhammad then said, "The witness was not credible." Unbelievable!

Getting in his two cents' worth, the Reverend Marcellus Harris said, "This whole thing toward Michael Vick amounts to subliminal racism." Whatever the heck that means! These two buffoons are classic examples of what black America does not need.

Thankfully, Louis Farrakhan is fading from view. His followers are still seen on the street corners hawking his hate propaganda toward whites, Christians, and Jews. The moniker that has been attached to Farrakhan is appropriate: "Hitler in a bow tie." The façade of a million men who are good citizens is a ruse to cover his twisted purposes. I can say assuredly that unlike Jesse Jackson, at least Farrakhan leaves no doubt as to whom and what he really is.

The race-baiters will perpetually keep racial tensions inflamed in America if we don't collectively refuse to tolerate it. Stand up. Don't be concerned about being labeled as a racist or bigot when you know that's not true. If you and I don't, they will continue to pull us apart along racial lines and create a hatred for each other that will kill America.

Don't do as the race-baiters and judge an entire race of people by a few. Don't be intimidated by their hateful labels and divisive accusations. I learned a long time ago that you cannot stop people from saying things about you, but you have the power to keep it from being the truth.

Let's work to improve race relations without anybody feeling degraded. Let's work together from a positive position of mutual respect and dignity, lest America self-implode.

Chapter 5

A Loathing of Patriotism

Cloaked in Free Expression

—⟋⟍—

The clarion call for the loathers of patriotism is this: America is always wrong. America is oppressive. America is arrogant. America must be put in her place. Those who reject the concept of patriotism do so based on the premise of free expression. Thus, I'm free to despise this country, the flag, the national anthem, the Pledge of Allegiance, national pride, all of it. And *are* we free to do that? Yes! But should we? Should we make traitorous statements and act in a way that undermines our greatness and gives encouragement to our enemies?

When one has a loathing of these symbols of freedom, one also loathes the concepts, the laws, the structure, and the strength of freedom. America has become too free when we condone traitors.

Boy, I can hear the free-speech outlaws screeching at that statement! But like it or not, it's true. Traitors are people who enjoy freedom and all its protections and benefits; then they turn right around and trash objects of honor. They ridicule the established precepts that continue to provide them and the rest of us freedom. Cowards abuse freedom purchased by the blood of others. How dare they exhibit an ignorant bias toward liberty!

But you see, what these airheads don't understand is that a love for these symbols of freedom and freedom itself, and pride in being an American have driven men and women to fight and die to maintain this unique freedom that we so dearly cherish.

People don't fight and die for something they don't love. Unpatriotic people don't care about how we have secured freedom throughout history. They cloak themselves in the catch phrase *free expression,* believing that free expression carries with it no responsibility. Their actions and words are careless and reckless, justifying burning the flag, running down America, and mocking other people's patriotic displays.

I especially get angry at the way some of the so-called pop stars botch the national anthem at big events and embarrass those present.

When you ask, "Why do you do that?" they answer, "Because we're free to express ourselves." Fine! You are, but do that among people who have the same disrespect for America that you do.

Oh, we're free to express our loathing. Is that ridiculous or what? How did that kind of thinking ever come about? Does a degree come with acquiring that type of ignorance?

Listen, we cannot remain free as a nation if we don't teach younger generations to love their country, their freedom, the security, and the free enterprise freedom represents. We must set an example to honor the symbols that so plainly represent the internal makeup of America. The loathers of freedom denigrate the United States of America and think it's chic to be seen as experiencing freedom so fully and completely that they must attack every single patriotic emblem.

Let's examine that logic. That's like saying in order to experience the fullness of the right to possess money, I'll rob the bank to demonstrate that right. Ludicrous! Let's cut to the chase. It is never about experiencing the ultimate of free expression. It's about a growing, aggressive loathing of the greatness of America and all she stands for.

It is about a mind-set that takes great pleasure in mocking something so wonderful and complex that they simply can't understand what the rest of us can. As a heckler mocks a truthful speaker, it's about gleefully demeaning symbols that grateful Americans revere as objects of the proud history of who and what we are. I've watched protesters and flag burners, small-minded people who have no real purpose in life and who are frustrated at their own miserable existence. They derive a sick satisfaction from in-your-face demonstrations of disdain for America, somehow blaming their own life's failures on our country. They are cowards who will boldly demonstrate under police protection, but who would crawl under the bed, hide, and whimper if our land was invaded.

Do we honestly believe these people would ever fire a shot to defend this nation? No! They would gladly turn it over on a silver platter and lower our flag to the ground—a flag that stands for a distinct and treasured life that Americans are supposed to defend in order to ensure its continuance. But they would have the white flag ready at that moment in time, believing they have been instrumental in accomplishing something noble—jubilation at seeing America and her symbols brought down.

But you know what? When the glee wore off, the shock of lost freedom would set in. There would be the sudden realization that the loathing of freedom so wantonly expressed was the root cause of freedom's death, and it would be impossible to bear.

But here is the most glaring problem with loathers of freedom. In past and present wars, the military people who gave their lives were fighting enemies who held to the same evil thinking about our nation as these who so callously protest patriotism. It's the same kind of hatred. This is a new "hatriotism" by an internal enemy toward the balance of freedom in America.

Make no mistake; many of these anti-America people are from other countries, or they are people who have been brainwashed by cultures abroad that despise America. France is guilty as charged of using dissidents to sow discord among America's people, and they have been successful. France's behavior toward America has been ungrateful and shameful. Chirac, France's former leader, is a two-faced, money-grubbing liar who will do anything for money.

The following story epitomizes France's cavalier attitude toward America, but it is also vindicating. An elderly American gentleman arrived in Paris, France, by airplane. At French customs, he fumbled for his passport. "You 'ave been to Franze before, monsieur?" the customs officer asked sarcastically.

The old gent admitted he had been to France one time before. "Zen you should know enough to 'ave your passport ready for inspection."

The old gentleman said, "The last time I was here, I didn't have to show it."

"Impossible. You Americans alwayz 'ave to show your passports on arrival in Franze!"

The elderly American gave the arrogant Frenchman a long hard look. Then he explained, "Well, when I came ashore at Omaha Beach on D-Day in 1944, I couldn't find a Frenchman to show it to."

Maybe France is still mad because a strong, mighty, and fearless nation had to deliver them. You think?

No doubt about it. The most dangerous loathing of all is directed toward our military from the Hollywood kooks to the radical professors to the pacifist politicians and the socialist writers. This loathing has extremely dangerous consequences.

Cindy Sheehan has been the most recent mouthpiece and poster child for the Far Left military haters. Though I and others deeply sympathize with this poor woman for the loss of her son, her extreme actions of bitter hatred toward the president, the military, and America cannot be excused. Cindy Sheehan has not only disgraced herself as a grieving mother, but she has besmirched the memory of her son who died with honor doing what he wanted to do and what he believed in. She has shamed and humiliated her husband, her family, and her friends by protesting in the manner in which she did, even stooping so low as to embrace the dangerous dictator Venezuela's Hugo Chavez, a vicious America-hater.

Now, I believe that no one with an ounce of sense wants to see *anyone* die in a war, but sometimes it becomes necessary in order to protect our nation and ensure our right to live without fear of being terrorized by an aggressive and unprovoked enemy. This is an enemy of mindless killers who seek to destroy us and the families that we love.

Cindy Sheehan does not realize that she was used as a pawn by coldhearted, Far Left manipulators who capitalized on the pain that she felt from losing her son, and they fueled her emotion with antiwar rhetoric and high-volume screeching. The bottom line is, she was used as a pawn to embarrass the president and denigrate

America in the eyes of the world. And as soon as she became old news, she was relocated to the irrelevant file and left alone to suffer not only the loss of her child, but the added suffering of making a fool out of herself and losing the rest of her family.

Cindy Sheehan is not the first mother to lose a child in war, nor will she be the last. Reasonable Americans understand the concept that when men or women join the military, they join a fighting force that is trained to kill the enemy that threatens America. By accepting that responsibility, they understand that the danger of dying in battle is very real and ever present.

I have attended funerals where moms and dads buried a son or daughter who died in war, and they conducted themselves with honor even through their grief. We must understand that the call to Americans is to be patriots and to support our fighting forces, lest we take the heart and will out of those who have chosen this life of military service and who proudly defend America so that our children and grandchildren can sleep safely at night.

I was watching a Veterans Day parade last year. As I was standing on a street corner, I saw proud men go by, their shoulders bent with age, hair gray, and wearing uniforms of a time long ago. Some of the uniforms were rumpled and moth-eaten. Many of these old warriors for freedom were unable to walk. Some were riding on trucks. Some were being pushed in wheelchairs. One especially stood out.

He was walking, shuffling along, and carrying an old rifle on his shoulder. His head was held high, as high as he could muster the energy to do so. He proudly went along, trying to march to the military band. Sometimes he got his marching step mixed up.

As I stood with a lump in my throat, I overheard two twenty-something yuppie types laughing and mocking the parade. I quickly chastised them both and asked if they had any idea of what freedom is or the price these old warriors had paid for them to stand on that corner and speak without fear of death. I reminded them that many never even made it back home to be buried. What was so disturbing to me about that moment was the fact that this unfeeling loathing of our military, past and present, has permeated the minds of those who don't have enough common sense to know better or the insight to see where it will take us as a nation. Because without patriotism, America would not exist as it does today.

It came to my mind as I watched those veterans trudge slowly by that if the call to arms was issued, these same old vets on whom time and war had exacted its toll would again freely offer to defend our nation. An unknown author said, "Poor is the nation that has no heroes. Shameful is the one that having them forgets."

The antiwar crowd in this country portrays our armed forces as murderers instead of defenders, liabilities to our peace instead of liberators of the oppressed, ignoring the fact that they are men and women who work each day to ensure the safety of us all. The elite of America rail against military personnel on foreign fields of battle, characterizing them as aggressors and occupiers. What these narrow-minded geniuses won't even try to comprehend is this: if our armies were not over there fighting terrorism, they would be fighting it on the streets of America. That very real possibility always seems to escape know-it-alls. They just don't get it, and I don't hold out any hope that they ever will. This crowd is so blinded by a virulent loathing of the very element that holds and protects us as a united nation.

The hue and cry being echoed by dissidents, pacifists, and uninformed political candidates is that the United States made terrorist threats worse by invading Iraq. They wrongly believe that Saddam Hussein had nothing to do with terrorism.

Ernest Hollings, the retired liberal South Carolina senator, continues to blather the completely dishonest assessment that President George Bush has made terrorists hate us, trotting out a new Democratic weapon that President Bush has made matters worse. It won't work, Ernest. Thank you for retiring, as you told us you would.

Allow me to set the record straight. Osama bin Laden's family disowned him. Doing that was expedient in order to protect their international business interests throughout the world. Osama was banished because the Saudi Arabian leaders could no longer tolerate his terrorist activities and maintain their credibility in the world market.

Osama left Saudi Arabia and found safe haven in Afghanistan, which at the time was controlled by the maniacal Taliban, who were very sympathetic to his cause. I guess lunatics of a feather flock together. Osama's family froze his monetary assets, other than what he had hidden in foreign accounts. Now where, pray tell, did Osama get the continued millions to finance terrorism on such a global scale?

I submit, and so do many others in the region, that Saddam Hussein supplied a major portion of the money to finance terrorism. Would Saddam do that? This is the same Saddam who paid the parents of

Hamas families twenty-five thousand dollars every time one of their children died in a suicide bomb attack that killed Israelis.

Clear-thinking American people have made the connection, even without the presence of weapons of mass destruction. I am sure they were spirited away and disassembled, or sold to another outlaw regime. Most likely Abu Musab al-Zarqawi has been the go-between.

We have to get over the cluelessness. Terrorism did not just begin on September 11. It started twenty-five years ago. That's right! Muslim terrorists started killing Americans twenty-five years ago, with no provocation and for no other reason than they hate us, our freedom, our prosperity, and our God.

In November 1979, Iranians attacked the U.S. embassy in Tehran. This was an outright attack on American soil. Terrorists overran the embassy and took American citizens hostage, stupefying then president Jimmy Carter. Carter decided on a sneak attack through the desert, which failed miserably. Why did it fail? Because Jimmy Carter, the spineless wimp that he was, gave in to the howls of the liberal military-haters and made deep cuts in defense spending. The military was ill-financed, undercommitted, and morale was at an all-time low. Training was proven to be well below standard.

This attack was an omen of more attacks to come. It wouldn't be long before Muslim terrorists would start murdering Americans. In April of 1983, a truck packed with explosives rammed the U.S. embassy in Beirut. Sixty-three people died instantly. A little more than six months later, an armed vehicle carrying twenty-five hundred pounds of dynamite bulled its way into the U.S. Marines' camp head-quarters in Beirut, where 241 American military people were killed. Two months later in December 1983, an explosive-laden vehicle struck the U.S. embassy in Kuwait.

In September 1984, another attempt was made on the U.S. embassy in Beirut. In April 1985, Muslim terrorists set off an explosive device in a restaurant in Madrid. U.S. soldiers were the intended target. In August, a car filled with explosives hit the Rhein-Main Air Base and took the lives of twenty-two people.

In 1988, Pan Am Flight 103 was sabotaged and blown up over the Scottish highlands, killing all 259 aboard. In January of 1993, two members of the United States CIA operations were assassinated.

In February 1993, a Muslim terrorist cell hit the World Trade Center with a van loaded with explosives; six died.

In November 1995, a car bomb was detonated on a U.S. base in Riyadh, Saudi Arabia; seven died. In June 1996 at Dharan, Saudi Arabia, a vehicle bomb exploded. It destroyed a military barracks; nineteen died, and many more were hurt. More U.S. embassies located in Kenya and Tanzania were attacked, and 224 people died.

The *U.S.S. Cole* was docked in Yemen, a hotbed area for Muslim terrorists. A small boat was exploded at the hull of the U.S. ship, and seventeen navy personnel died.

Did we acknowledge that Muslim terrorists were trying to kill us? No, we did not. The military-loathers refused to accept the fact that an ominous pattern was developing. Then on September 11, 2001, a well-organized cell of Muslim terrorists hijacked commercial airliners, plowing them deep into the World Trade Center towers and the Pentagon. Over 3,000 innocent American citizens, some drinking coffee at their desks, died horribly.

Hello! Wake up! We have done nothing as a nation, nor will we do anything, as some claim, to rile the Muslim world against us. They have been beating the war drums toward America for years.

To even for a moment make that claim shows how delusional the loathers of freedom are.

Blind haters of the military had weakened our intelligence and alertness to how great the threat really was. We never took into consideration twenty-five years of attacks and murders. They were incredulously discounted, and looking the other way finally culminated in the unthinkable.

The antipatriots and the antimilitary establishment have now politicized their loathing, and freedom hangs in the balance. Martin Sheen, Susan Sarandon, Barbara Streisand, Sean Penn, and the limousine liberals of the blame-the-United States-first organization have taken their frothing-at-the-mouth loathing to the point that their actions have now placed America's citizens and fighting forces in peril. What makes it so bad is, they don't care.

Over the years, I have lived in close proximity to two air force bases. I have had people ask me, "Does the noise of the planes flying overhead bother you, especially at night?" I answer this way, "No. When I hear the roar of those jets it's a comforting sound. It's the sound of freedom."

As long as those jets are flying, I know we are still free. As long as I can see a navy ship cutting through the sea or men marching on training bases, I know we're still free. As long as Old Glory is flying on a flagpole, that's a reassuring sign that we are free. When we hear a true version of the national anthem belted out, it brings goose bumps of freedom and national pride.

We need a revival of patriotism in our country. You see, it's still true today, to whom much is given, much is required. America has enjoyed a life of freedom that others in the world only dream of. But with this freedom comes a serious charge to use our freedom responsibly and stand at the ready to defend it at all cost, both from enemies within and without. If we shirk our duty to our country, then a loathing of patriotism cloaked in freedom will imprison us in chains fashioned by free expression, and our nation will be no more.

Chapter 6

Religion's Spiritual Failings

Cloaked in a Holy Garment

I n *Walden*, Henry David Thoreau wrote, "There is no odor so bad as that which arises from goodness tainted." How true! As spirituality declines in America, so do moral values. The present state of a large percentage of religion in America is as Thoreau described: *tainted*. The concept of religious people being the salt of the earth seems to have gotten lost over the years. Slowly but surely, religion has lost its purpose.

I read a story about a man who owned a fish market. He placed a sign in his window that read *Fresh Fish for Sale*. Someone came along and said, "Everybody knows your fish is fresh; remove the word *fresh*." So the fishmonger did.

The sign then read *Fish for Sale*. Soon another person said, "Why do you have *for Sale* on your sign? Everyone knows that you are not giving the fish away." So the seller obliged, and the sign simply read *Fish*.

At last a man prevailed upon the seller to remove the sign that read *Fish*. Reasoning that people knew what he sold and there was no need for a sign, the man went out of business in two weeks.

That describes much of religion today—still there, but virtually gone out of business. So much has been removed from true worship that nothing spiritual is left. Why? Because slowly but surely the tenets of faith that separate biblical religion from every other group and make God's religion stand out are being taken away at the suggestion of people who know nothing about what God wants or expects from His church.

A prime example is what a number of churches opted to do on December 25, 2006, when Christmas happened to fall on Sunday. Christmas on Sunday—what an awesome opportunity to invite unchurched people to come and hear the true story of Christ's birth! What a wonderful time for Christians to actually be *in* church on the day that the world celebrates the birth of God's Son! This is a time to sing "Joy to the World" together.

Surely God would be pleased at such an opportunity for people to worship Him during the most commercialized day of the year. One would think that the religious houses of worship would not join in on the commercialization of history's greatest Christian event. But many churches throughout America *closed their doors that day.* They shut out the world from a potential spiritual blessing for life.

Why in the world would those who have been given the charge to go into the highways and hedges and compel them to come in pass up such a prime time in which to demonstrate goodwill to all men? I'll tell you why. Religious political correctness; in other words, these church leaders and their limp-wristed, spineless reverends wanted to be viewed as churches that take their *cue* from society rather than being the *cure* for society's ills. They chose to not accept the divine call to be bright and shining lighthouses in a world that is fast becoming comfortable with spiritual darkness.

I shudder to think how many people on that Christmas Day would have sought solace from maybe spending their first Christmas without a mate, without a child, without a mom or dad, or who were just plain lonely. If only the doors had been opened, they could have received a smile, a hug, an encouraging word, and a verse of Scripture that could have consoled and made a life-changing impact. Considering the commitment or lack thereof of those closed-door churches, I guess it's possible that it's better to be lonely than in the presence of people who take the work of the church and the love of God so lightly.

Modern people today do not believe the church can be counted on to do the right thing. Once Christ's church in America distinguished itself as above reproach. Now, too many times, the church is reproachful.

The church is commissioned to be salt. Salt influences, preserves, and changes whatever it is added to. It's clear that religious salt is powerless to influence a changing America. The fear of being politically incorrect has paralyzed some of those who should set the standard for values and purity, and they yield instead to external pressure resulting in an emerging social message. A self-help philosophy is being hailed as a religious breakthrough, when what people actually need and are seeking is *divine help*.

It is dangerous for the church to become popular with the world it serves because the church loses its righteous character. Just having the right programs or religiously entertaining people is not spiritual substance. People are starving for something that will make a lasting difference in life. Churchgoers are confused. It's hard to make the distinction between a ministry that is true and one that is false.

Scandals, child molestations, and the like have marked the last twenty years of religious life in America. Too many churches have lost their divine direction. People who are hurting are reaching out to someone they believe they can trust and should be able to trust. Wolves in sheep's clothing that are savagely tearing innocent lambs to pieces are betraying these trusting souls. To quote Warren Wiersbe from his book *The Integrity Crisis*, "The priests and false prophets peddle a popular brand of religion that gives people enough religious experience to make them happy, but not enough truth to make them holy."

That statement was made in 1988 and has proven to be prophetic. Religion today makes it easy for people to feel great, embrace sinful practices that destroy a person's being, and adopt the philosophy "Do others before they do you."

There are many genuine and sincere men of God in America who give their lives to serve humankind, but unfortunately, there are others who don't. George Whitefield once said something like this: "God can send a nation of people no greater blessing than to give them faithful, sincere, and upright ministers, and the greatest curse that God can allow upon a people is to give them over to the blind, unregenerate, carnal, lukewarm, and unskilled guides." Yet we find that throughout the ages, there have been many wolves in sheep's clothing who spoke and did things God did not allow.

Raphael was painting his famous Vatican frescoes when two cardinals stopped, watched a while, and then criticized. "The face of the apostle Paul is too red," said one. Raphael replied, "He blushes to see into whose hands the church has fallen." Today we observe false religions controlling members' minds and taking their money, while giving empty promises of wealth and healing.

I read about a young woman, the mother of two children, who died from loss of blood. Her religion taught against blood transfusions, and her husband refused to let her have the procedure, though doctors said it was necessary in order to save her life. That is not religion; it's lunacy. She did not have to die and leave her children crying for their mother.

Some churches are providing blessings for cats and dogs, while parishioners are starving for spiritual attention. Other religions institute horrible man-devised rules that oppress and frighten, while providing teen girls as wives for lecherous men. Some religions never allow their followers to know God. The leaders set themselves up as earthly gods, convincing people that they must go through them in order to pray or worship the one true God. Other leaders use minority churches as incubators for political activism, ordaining every politi-cian so that they have the title *reverend*. I guess that is supposed to make them legitimate and make the huge love offerings (campaign contributions) legal so the IRS tax laws are circumvented.

Religion should impact our society with principles and precepts that add stability, harmony, and joy to our lives, while denouncing sinful acts that destroy precious lives. Thankfully, there are many that do. They actually have the best interest of people at heart. Their ministries are designed to minister and support missions work all over the world, thereby satisfying the spiritual hunger of people of all ages.

A church should be a safe haven for those who are seeking to fill a void in life, not a place to be hurt, disillusioned, and confused about who God and His Son really are. Reprehensible actions by wayward supposed servants and pastors have left worshippers with empty cups and tear-stained faces.

I would be remiss if I did not point out the "boss run" churches, churches that are run by a couple of families who believe they are somehow better than everybody else. They try to convince others that they have cornered the market on all things spiritual, and God has chosen to speak expressly to them. These self-appointed religious lynch mobs have destroyed many a church and broken the hearts of sincere pastors.

Then you have the fighting churches, those who fight over every single issue. You can draw a larger crowd for a Wednesday night business meeting than you can for an Easter worship service. They live to argue, fuss, and blast one another. Woe to any pastor unfortunate enough to be called by these religious imposters!

America has a right to expect integrity, character, honesty, and truth within religion. From most, we are not receiving that. What we are receiving is corruption, lies, sex scandals, the dismantling of long-held beliefs and faith foisted on us by religious leaders devoid of divineness to guide us to heights of spiritual truth and godliness. Most are fakes, phonies, and charlatans tainted by a lust of the eyes, a lust of the flesh, and the pride of life.

Lately I have observed religious leaders perverting the doctrines of their own religion and ripping their denominations apart. Look, if you want to have a religion that is permissive and makes a mockery of the tenets of your faith, then go start your own, just as Jimmy Carter did with the help of Bill Clinton. Carter wants to improve the Baptist image, but unfortunately, his religious image is the one that desperately needs improving. On the other hand, he did improve the Southern Baptist image when he left that denomination to form a group that would embrace his more liberal religious philosophy.

Don't try to force your unsound views on your religion. Be respectful! Why is it necessary to elicit the stamp of approval from people who disagree with you?

Gene Robinson, the former leader of the Episcopal Church, is a classic example. Here is a guy who crushes his wife emotionally, embarrasses his children, and if that were not reprehensible enough, he wages war on his religion by becoming the centerpiece to throw out a doctrine that is clear in Scripture and one the Episcopals have embraced for a hundred years: that of condemning homosexuality. Why? His self-indulgent pursuit is more important to him than respect for others and the truth. This nitwit needs to find an honest living, because calling himself a minister is certainly not honest.

Too many religious leaders are self-serving and ego-driven. They simply do not have the best interest in mind for those they are serving or the God they are professing to worship.

A growing number of pastors and priests have allowed themselves to become moral cowards. They feel safe and secure in their own churches but lack the fortitude for the fight that is required of pastors to influence America with the values that have sustained us for two hundred years. These timid of heart will not defend their flocks from the advancing hordes of immorality, indecency, perversion, and wickedness. They choose instead to retreat to the temporary safety of their studies, leaving parishioners to figure it all out and fend for themselves.

Another aspect of church life that is troubling is this: most grassroots church members have no idea what their denominations do with the money. More often than not, a portion is doled out supporting causes and social issues that would shock the folks back home in the local assembly.

The cloaked church in America is fast becoming corporate religiosity, or what I call *churchianity*. I have discovered that some of the most callous businessmen and businesswomen in America are executives in certain denominations, ruling with iron fists and collecting huge speaking fees by virtue of the positions held in the religious hierarchy of these respective denominations.

The National Council, the World Council of Churches, and their agenda-maddened leaders are prime examples of religion gone sour. They have been caught with their hands in the proverbial cookie jar, supporting Muslim charities that were set up to finance so called Freedom Fighter training camps, and they knew it. They have fanned the flames of anti-American sentiment all over the world while cloaking themselves in the word *church*.

Both organizations have a solid track record of coming down on the wrong side of every issue that is detrimental both to the United States and to conservative Christianity. I can safely say that the mission purpose is to finance radical causes, both politically and religiously, all around the globe. These efforts undermine democracy and discredit reputable religious work. They are contrary to the moral values that you would expect from a group using the word *church* in its name.

The Presbyterian Church U.S.A. is perhaps the worst mainline denomination in America, and they do everything from advocating abortion and gay marriage, and supporting Planned Parenthood to literally taking churches away from the congregations that built them. But who didn't read the fine print in the denominational contract, wording that gave the PCUSA (Presbyterian Church U.S.A.) the power to take control of the property if the congregation dared stand against their religious liberalism? They have consistently lobbied for economic sanctions against Israel. They want to literally starve this tiny nation to death. Why? In their liberal religious minds, they believe Israel is the source of the Middle East's unrest.

To arrive at that conclusion, you have to stretch your thinking beyond being sane. The PCUSA was time and again supportive of Yasser Arafat's murderous regime, a regime that even after his death continues to brag about the successes of the Holocaust. This regime kills every innocent Jew in sight. The PCUSA is a religious-front organization and has lost its moral compass, adrift in a sea of religious evil, claiming to worship a God they know nothing of. May true worshippers be delivered from the clutches of any church that lowers itself to the point that it no longer understands a ministry of righteousness.

The spiritual values that traditional Presbyterians have strongly held for decades are not the values that the PCUSA is putting forth today. The powers to be in the PCUSA recently adopted a gender-neutral change in defining the Holy Trinity of Father, Son, and Holy Spirit as Rock, Redeemer, and Friend. This type of ridiculous tampering with Scripture is met with shock and disbelief by the local churches of the PCUSA.

These denominational leaders are religious pirates who have boarded the ships of their respective denominations, looted the true principles and precepts of Scripture, and replaced them with religious nonsense. My advice to the local parishioners is to change your denomination's control or get out as fast as you can.

We should be grateful to the churches and pastors who *are* true to their callings by supporting them with our attendance, service, and money. We should never lump everybody together; that would be wrong. We as Americans would cheat ourselves out of the positive impact that God can have on our personal lives, marriages, and homes. We need to be faithful to those who have remained faithful to a holy God. We should remain loyal to those who have not dipped their flags into the mud of a secular sewer.

Sure, many people are skeptical and weary of the scandals and the soiled reputation of religion. That is the reason 40 percent of Americans feel they can no longer safely rely on religion to be upright. Why? Religion has, it seems, proved time and time again to sell its soul for a bowl of pottage.

Teens and young adults are the largest group disenfranchised. It just doesn't compute with them that a real church has substance. Instead, alcohol, drugs, premarital sex, and idols will fill the void that is left in each young life.

The most disturbing aspect of the present state of a large segment of religion today is the underlying motives that are carefully cloaked in an aura of the holy. Churches and men of God soil their ministries and testimonies before a nation of people who desperately need divine guidance now more than ever before in history, who need the lighthouse that is supposed to be God's church guiding people safely to a secure place in life.

I read a story of the tiny ermine, a small animal whose fur is snow-white. The ermine's fur is sought after and coveted by kings and royalty because its fur is a symbol of the utmost purity. Men capture the ermine by waiting until the little animal leaves its burrow in the trunk of a tree, and then they smear blackened foul-smelling grease all around the entrance. When the men begin to chase the ermine, the animal will run to its burrow. Upon finding the opening smeared with filth, the ermine will not enter and chooses instead to be captured. Its captors will then kill this courageous, little animal. The ermine would rather die with blood on its pure coat of fur than live with one soiled with filth.

Religion in America could learn a great lesson from the ermine. Stand and fight for the purity of the gospel of God rather than be soiled by the filth of impurity.

Alexis de Tocqueville, the famous nineteenth-century French statesman, historian, and social philosopher, came to America in the 1830s to search and write about the reasons for the prosperity of the newly birthed country. He penned his findings in two volumes, *Democracy in America*. He was deeply moved by the spiritual life that he observed throughout America. After searching for America's greatness, here is what he discovered and wrote:

Upon arrival in the United States, the religious aspect of the country was the first thing that struck my attention, and the longer I stayed there, the more I perceived the great political consequences resulting from this new state of things.

In France I had almost always seen the spirit of religion and the spirit of freedom marching in opposite directions. But in America I found they were intimately united and that they reigned in common over the country. Religion in America . . . must be regarded as the foremost of the political institutions of that country, for if it does not impart a taste of freedom, it facilitates the use of it. Indeed it is in the same point of view that the inhabitants of the United States themselves look upon religious belief.

I do not know whether all Americans have a sincere faith in their religion—for who can search the human heart? But I am certain that they hold it to be indispensable to the maintenance of republican institutions. This opinion is not peculiar to a class of citizens or a party, but it belongs to the whole nation and to every rank of society.

In the United States, the sovereign authority is religion. There is no country in the world where the Christian religion retains a greater influence over the souls of men than in America, and there can be no greater proof of its utility and of its conformity to human nature than that influence is powerfully felt over the most enlightened and free nation of the earth.

In the United States, the influence of religion is not confined to the manners, but it extends to the intelligence of the people. . . . Christianity therefore reigns without obstacle, by universal consent.

I sought for the key to greatness and genius of America in the harbors . . . in her fertile fields and boundless forests, in her rich mines and vast world commerce, in her public school system and institutions of learning. I sought for it in her democratic Congress and her matchless Constitution. Not until I went into the churches of America and heard her pulpits aflame with righteousness did I understand the secret of her genius and power. America is great because America is good, and if America ever ceases to be good, America will cease to be great.

May religion in America never forget that powerful and wonderful observation.

The absence of a religious moral compass will slowly ruin America, because no one else or any institution can fill the void in the human heart that the church is called to fill.

Chapter 7

The Gay Agenda

Cloaked as an Alternative Lifestyle

—∿∿—

What causes a person to be gay? Is it genetics? No, Biblically it is learned immoral behavior, like any other immoral behavior. Leading geneticists in America debunk the theory that gays are born that way. Not one single gene has ever been identified to link a person's being gay to a gene at birth that predestines homosexuality. Therefore, the argument that a person is gay and has no choice is without merit. However, I never could understand that if being gay is supposed to be a good thing, why do gays want sympathy, special attention, and pity?

That being said, here is the problem that I have with the gay agenda: If people want to be gay, then okay, nobody is going to stop them. What they do in private is their own business, but when gays want millions of people who happen to believe that the homosexual lifestyle is reprehensible, to accept them as normal, and when gays try to force the public to change their beliefs to accommodate the gay agenda, that is wrong; and this is the point where the trouble starts.

You see, if I decide to believe that homosexuality is wrong, I am not going to allow you to say I have a phobia—that's my right! There is nothing that tells me that I am compelled to tolerate a life-style that I personally abhor.

If we closely examine the gay lifestyle, then we see a much different picture than the "guy-and-gal-next-door" gay agenda puts forth. Most homosexuals have an average of fifteen partners a year. The vast majority of homosexuals are opposed to same-sex marriage, and they don't mind saying so. Why? Marriage among gays would bring too much unwanted attention to their hopping from partner to partner.

Even in Massachusetts, where gay marriages were legalized beginning in 2005, the number of gay marriages plunged after the initial euphoria wore off, because they obviously would rather have their one-night stands than be committed to one partner. One gay man said that gay marriage would bore him to death. It's been found that the most committed gay couples could not maintain sexual faithfulness beyond four years. It's clear the gay agenda wants the benefit of marriage, but with no personal commitment. It's also clear that they want to create a subculture in America by reducing heterosexual marriage to the same level as perversion.

The promiscuous lifestyle embraced by gays develops personality disorders leading to emotional instability. Homosexuals commit suicide at a rate ten times the national average. The homosexual's choice—and it is a choice—to have multiple relationships leads to violence and even murder. It is a widely accepted fact that homosexuals have higher rates of alcoholism, depression, drug abuse, and domestic violence than heterosexuals.

The greatest threat to the gay lifestyle is the proliferation of AIDS. One gay man who had given up gay activities told me that nine out of ten gay men have four to five stranger sexual encounters each week, and most don't use protection. That is the height of irresponsibility, but it is indicative of how this lifestyle consumes the reasonable thought processes of its participants. Again, that's their private business, and they are aware of the consequences.

Now let's list the problems that 69 percent of Americans have with radical homosexuality. The incessant chorusing is designed to badger the straight American public into submitting and accepting behavior that they find repugnant. People have had it with being accused of hating just because they exercise the right to judge homosexual behavior as deviant and those who participate in it as men and women who possess and exhibit a twisted view of human sexuality.

But gays, driven by their agenda, are not satisfied to live their lives and leave the rest of us alone. They want to shock the sensibilities of those of us who are not gay with public displays of debauchery that go well beyond the pale. The in-your-face, *I'm gay and you* **will** *like it* attitude is the root cause of the gay backlash in America.

Just recently two radical gays in San Francisco, California decided to boldly desecrate a Catholic church service. These two infidels were dressed for effect as they exhibited a blatant disregard for the church, the elderly priest and the people who had gone to worship.

Their intent was to mock God, embarrass people and cause disruption. But they also succeeded in enraging Americans.

Those of us who see gays as human beings who have morally lost their identities feel sympathy for them, realizing they are wayward individuals who are in serious need of a reality check. We view gays as we would someone who is hooked on cocaine. We wish gays no ill will, but not to the point that we accept perversion as normal. Acceptance of homosexuality has destroyed every society throughout history that has given in to it.

The thing I find most appalling is the attempt by gays to garner special rights by comparing their fight to legitimize *unnatural affection* to the same fight African Americans waged to secure equal rights. That is like stretching a bungee cord from the east coast to the west coast. You can try all you want, but there is a huge difference between how far it will actually stretch compared with how far you want it to stretch. Let me state clearly: *there is no comparison.* Forget that! No rational person is buying that. Every homosexual is protected by the same laws and rights that we all have.

Make no mistake; the gay agenda is not about rights. It's about sewing deviant behavior into the fabric of society and pretending it belongs. It's about silencing dissenting speech by attempting to legislate as hate language anything anyone dares say about being gay as morally wrong, putrid, and repulsive. Hello! It's about radical gays imposing an acceptance of behavior that 69 percent of America deems deplorable.

The driving force behind the gay rights movement in America is not just *Tolerate me* or *Let's live and let live;* they want a special recognition. They want perversion to have a coveted place in our schools as an alternate lifestyle.

Ted Kennedy and Chuck Schumer have authorized the Employment Nondiscrimination Act. The heart of this bill is to force the teaching of homosexuality on young children. If passed, this act would mandate that principals hire sexual predators, twisted people who are bent on legalizing sex between children and adults, to teach our nation's children.

As a parent, if you protested, you would be branded a bigot, and in order for your child to remain in school, you, the innocent, decent, moral parent, would have to attend a sensitivity class. The radical gays demonstrate a militant attitude that says, *We have the right to come in to your schools and destroy your children's innocence and moral foundation and steal them into the lurid world that is homosexuality. We'll do that by convincing children and teens that it is just another way. It's cool.*

Be forewarned: the gay agenda is fashioned to actively recruit children. Some gay and liberal educators and their sympathizers are making it easy for them to do so. Remember! Gay men don't have little gays—they recruit them. Gay women don't birth gay little girls—they indoctrinate them. The Man-Boy Love Society and other radical organizations that propose to destroy America's children physically, emotionally, and sexually are not decent people, no matter what they claim. All of us have the right to go our own way and make our own decisions. However, truly decent people never go after innocent children. If we as Americans don't stand up to this new onslaught of corruption from this dark part of our society, whose minds are inflamed with incorporating abhorrent behavior into our daily lives and calling it alternative, acceptable, and moral, then like a cancer, it will eat away at the moral wellness of America.

Over the last forty years, I have witnessed what this "alternative lifestyle" has done, both to those who are caught up in its tentacles and the innocent who have been devastated by its effects. Don't ever allow anyone to tell you it is a victimless pursuit. I have witnessed the broken hearts, the ruined futures, the shattered lives, and the untimely deaths of men and women who made a conscious and willful choice to enter the seedy world of homosexuality. I have felt the tears burn my face as I looked into the eyes of precious little children whose childhoods have been ripped from them. I have seen the vacant stares of the young who have been betrayed and violated by homosexuals who succumbed to their deviant personalities to the point that they could make no distinction between other adult homosexuals and lamblike children.

There will be no remedy for our nation if we allow homosexuality to ever be considered normal. Forget the howls and the screeching that we are homophobes and bigots. Name-calling must never deter us from reducing homosexuality to that of a man or woman's moral failing.

The hot new topic for homosexuals is gay marriage. Again they are cloaking. The ultimate goal is to destroy the cultural tradition of male and female marriage. It is apparent to most of America that homosexuals have a bitter hatred of traditional marriage. They preach tolerance, yet refuse to coexist with straight marriage. These perverts think everybody should be gay, and you are hateful if you are not.

A recent Gallup poll found that 62 percent of Americans oppose gay marriage. That is an overwhelming majority. By 72 percent, the voters in the state of Missouri recently voted to ban gay marriage. That is a landslide. It is proof positive that America is opposed to gay marriage. Missouri presently has laws defining marriage as just between a man and a woman. That means nothing to the radical gay activists who attempted to use an emotional appeal to garner enough votes to change the law.

So how does the gay agenda propose to legalize it? Through liberal, biased judges who will by judicial fiat foist the tenets of gay marriage on millions of objecting Americans. Liberal judges are attempting to redefine one of the fundamental cornerstones of American society: marriage as a union between a man and a woman. Thankfully, the California Supreme Court stopped the madness of gay marriage by ruling it illegal.

Listen, if anybody is so naïve as to believe that redefining marriage can happen without dire effects on our society, then those people are prime candidates to purchase a lake lot on Mars. Gay marriage will open a Pandora's box of free-speech violations. Any citizen who states a moral objection will be vilified as a purveyor of hatred. Churches can be sued, and pastors will lose radio and television programs.

A pastor in Europe was speaking about the biblical precepts condemning homosexuality when he was attacked and beaten mercilessly. When the police arrived, they arrested the pastor. Could that happen in America? You be the judge.

We also need to learn a lesson from our neighbors to the north. Canada has already declared that pastors who preach on radio programs cannot speak out against homosexuality. If they do, then those pastors are guilty of hate speech and are banned from the airwaves and fined. Almost immediately after gay marriage was ratified in Canada, the gay-agenda liberals passed bill C-250, making it a criminal offense to speak publicly and express that homosexuality is wrong. The penalty levied can be up to two years in prison. That's a precursor to dictatorship against morality.

You see, the gay-agenda platform is built on tolerance, but we see that they don't demonstrate tolerance. Marriage is not just confined to a mutual attraction between two people. Marriage is about the future of human society and its propagation. Now what transpired in Canada will come to pass in America, and the well-cloaked gay-agenda leaders know it. Churches will no longer have the religious freedom to put forth the biblical definition of marriage. In an

America fashioned by the gay agenda, both concepts of marriage will be predetermined as equal, and churches will then be expected to honor gay marriage as being the same as the biblical description of marriage. If they can secure the right to marry, they are achieving the goal that says a perverted marriage is as normal as a man-woman marriage; but it's not.

A home built around two homosexuals is proven by leading clinical psychologists to be dysfunctional and fraught with pitfalls. However, a greater danger than that looms. The bedrock on which a stable society is built is a *dad-and-mom home*, but when the bedrock cracks and the foundation turns to mud, our society and our way of life will slide into the hog pen of existence.

I don't accept the gays' argument that because some heterosexual marriages fail, then that must be a flawed concept of marriage. That's ridiculous! We as reasonable people cannot even attempt to justify bad behavior by pointing to other bad behavior. That won't cut it. Wrong can never be used to justify other wrong, at least not in a civilized society.

Gay rights advocates want churches to throw out long-held doctrines and religious beliefs and embrace what most religions in America call sodomy. Why must gays always want to force the issue? You believe what you want to. Don't compel me to change my religious doctrine to accommodate your skewed view of that which is wholesome and acceptable. Don't think that you can somehow cloak your lifestyle so that it becomes compatible with my religion. Go start your own churches, as some have. Say what you want to, but don't ridicule me and others just because we absolutely refuse to see religious permissiveness as you see it.

Please get this: if the U.S. Senate ratifies gay marriage, it will set a legal precedent that will literally invite unscrupulous lawyers to come after anybody—you, me, and anybody. We cannot allow this legislation to ever pass.

Another detrimental effect is the threat to fatherhood and motherhood. As Kathleen Parker of the *Orlando Sentinel* wrote, "Fathers don't think same-sex marriage affects them directly. In the light of the travails endured by the fatherhood movement over the past decade, same-sex marriage stands as a particularly decisive blow in the disenfranchisement of fathers in American life." How? By reinforcing the idea that one parent is disposable, which has been both an unspoken tenet in American divorce and the driving force behind the fathers' rights movement.

Parker further states that "it is in the best interest of a child to have a mother and a father; that same-sex marriage is assumed on two faulty premises: that children do not need both a mother and a father, that two moms or two dads are just as good as a mother and a father." She also says, "We who have reared children know better. The unique gifts that a mother and father bring to their children cannot be replaced by same-sex substitutes, and children have an equal right to have both a mother and father." Mrs. Parker is right on target and courageous to say so. As she predicts, she will be called a bigot because of her willingness to speak the truth.

It is tragic that opposite beliefs about an issue that has so much potential to destroy an ordered society have been discoursed through intimidation and name-calling. But that's the way the gay-agenda leaders operate. They are so blinded by their moral lapse that they refuse to acknowledge that instability in a home wrecks children's security, causing them to lose their own identities in the world in which they live. Children are embarrassed when their friends see them living with two men or two women, and it emotionally scars them for life.

The homosexual lifestyle is selfish in that homosexuals are both heartless as to what their deviant behavior does to the innocent and self-destructive in how they waste the life that is given to them and eventually die in a self-created moral sewer.

The gay agenda people will never be satisfied to just live their lifestyle. I am convinced of that. They want everybody in America to embrace the concept that nothing is wrong with being gay, and it has no adverse consequences. But that is far removed from the actual truth. Radical homosexuals are always going to be mocking, ridiculing, and attacking those of us who even remotely oppose the gay agenda. But if history is a good professor—and it is—and if the American people allow this hidden agenda cloaked as an innocent, alternative lifestyle, then radical homosexuality will draw blood deep from the heart of our nation.

Chapter 8

Liberal Media Bias

Cloaked as Responsible Journalism

—⁕—

L et's begin with this question: is there a liberal media bias? Of course there is, but those who work in the liberal media say it is simply a "perceived liberal bias." In other words, you and I don't really understand what we are hearing. No, Dorothy, you're not in news fantasyland any longer. There is a liberal media bias, comprised of left-wing bomb throwers who become infuriated at any news that does not meet their approval or, God forbid, anybody else's opinion that differs from their own.

The shameful acts they employ to discredit credible news organizations or news anchors run the gamut from personal attacks to smear campaigns, character assassinations, and downright slander. They will descend to any depths in order to defend liberal and biased news coverage. This classless and hateful bunch will say anything to defend their stated position. I have found that the liberal media never wants to be confused by facts. Reality seems too difficult for them to process.

Most Americans can no longer trust the biased liberal media. When news is reported honestly, then they can decide for themselves. The liberal media have become newsmakers instead of responsible journalists who are identified by their honesty to report the news. Instead, the liberal media have opted to slant and spin breaking news. They filter it and do rewrites in order to achieve their social purposes. The liberal media arrogantly justify all things liberal this way: if we don't make the news as we interpret it to be, then the balance will be lost and there is no objectivity. That's preposterous! That's like saying too much truth is just not a good thing, so we must seed it with some lies.

The general public has rejected this concept of journalism. Am I correct? Well, consider this: Rush Limbaugh, even with all his fallacies and self-inflicted problems, still has 14.5 million weekly listeners. What accounts for that? The man will present the facts. He respects his listeners' right to decide. He has no hidden agenda. Just tell the truth, and the American people have enough sense to digest it and appropriate it accordingly. But the liberal media hate Limbaugh because he dares expose them and he breaks up the bias party.

Fox News's findings indicate they have 1.3 million prime-time viewers. Why? People trust them to be truthful, fair, and balanced, not biased. Bill O'Reilly is continually maligned by the liberal media because he has become the champion of the average American. He pulls the cloaks aside and exposes lies and distortions of current events. He refuses to be a mouthpiece for either political party, choosing instead to represent truth and the people who are responsible for his popularity.

Paul Krugman, a columnist for the *New York Times,* has of late, with his paranoid delusions, made a career of attacking Bill O'Reilly. This pompous, vile little man spews poison at conservatives such as O'Reilly, much as a spitting cobra spits poison; but with the cobra, you know what to expect. Krugman passes himself off as a respectable journalist who wants people to take him seriously, but he is so far left he is almost off the scale. Every time he writes about anything, if you are knowledgeable of his subject, you will be hard-pressed to find any truth in it, but you can find plenty of fabrications and distortions. He has earned the reputation among his colleagues as a man who will resort to any means to prove his own point of view, even if that means trashing those he opposes.

Writers like Krugman; Stuart Smalley; Thomas Oliphant of the *Boston Globe;* Tom Teepen of the *New York Times* and Maureen Dowd of the *New York Times;* Hendrich Herzberg, writer for the *New Yorker* magazine; and Cynthia Tucker, editor of the *Atlanta Constitution,* are prime examples of rank liberals who demonstrate bias without any conscience.

Moveon.org, *Media Matters*, and the *Daily Kos* are extremely dangerous secular progressive websites. They spew hate, smear good people who hold to traditional values, and propose a secular philosophy that would redefine America as a nation without principle and absolutes. It's a nation in their own image!

After the turnover of Iraq to the new Iraqi government, a strange occurrence took place that evening. Every person who tuned in to CBS or ABC television with Dan Rather and Peter Jennings respectively saw both men subdued and sullen. Why? The left-wing media that they so successfully represented were angry that things had not gone badly. There is no other way to describe it. It was glaringly evident. Both Rather and Jennings could not conceal their obvious displeasure that the turnover would be completed properly.

Again, why would two high-profile anchors display such shocking behavior? Simple answer! They did not want President Bush to look good in any way. Because the handover was done earlier than expected, the left-wing media liberals didn't have time to distort the event and spin it beforehand. That missed opportunity left them bitter toward the president. Their disdain for George Bush was blatant, even to the most casual observer.

But wait a minute! Isn't the media supposed to report the news to the American people as it is? Why would they subdue and downplay hopeful news, knowing that American military lives might be saved and the war not prolonged? Both Rather and Jennings were aware of the statement Prime Minister John Howard of Australia said so aptly: "If this experiment fails, if the terrorists win, the cost around the world, the boost it will give to terrorism around the world, will be quite incalculable." I'll tell you why. Liberal media icons like Rather are so blinded by liberal prejudice that they can no longer discern what is news-reporting and what is blatant bias and journalistic dishonesty.

Peter Jennings was a Canadian who was part atheist and part America-basher. His disrespect for this country was unwarranted—a country, by the way, that made him wealthy. His bias drew the attention of millions of Americans and Christians who stopped watching his broadcast even before he died. Jennings demonstrated clearly what his personal bias was when he would not allow Toby Keith to perform a song during an ABC special. This particular song referred to America's military putting a boot in the rear of terrorists. But you know what? The American people loved the song. It became a national battle cry. Jennings revealed plainly that he was out of touch with the majority of Americans.

Dan Rather, on the other hand, is just a dyed-in-the-wool liberal media Democrat who pouted and cried for a month while screaming Al Gore lost the election to George Bush—especially after he prematurely announced that Bush had won Florida before the polls even closed, thus sending thousands of Bush supporters home from long lines at voting places in the Florida panhandle. Rather, I believe, actually used his position to influence the outcome. Rather whines and becomes indignant about his truly loving America, yet he continues to put forth every liberal policy that he can. Hey, Dan! Most Americans don't agree with you.

It is journalists like these—and I use the word *journalist* loosely when applying it to Rather—who routinely cloak themselves as credible journalists. If truth be known, Rather has a malady I call "left-wing liberal media madness disease." Fortunately, Dan's playing fast and loose with the truth finally caught up with him when he ran a story about President Bush's National Guard service that was so blatantly untrue that the network, faced with mounting outrage and ridicule, was forced to do damage control and fire Dan. It was a good decision in support of honest journalism.

News anchor Katie Couric has taken up where Dan left off. She's exhibiting a sullen and arrogant liberal bias that is sending her ratings through the studio floor. I predict Couric will soon be gone as well. America is tiring of the bias.

When Tom Brokaw was with NBC, he was a well-respected newsman. Now NBC can no longer be trusted to bring the American people the truth. The network's twisted and biased reporting on Iraq is inexcusable, no matter what the powers to be at that network personally think of President Bush. Just tell it like it is, as Howard Cosell used to say, not like you want the public to believe that it is.

Bob Hebert of the *New York Times* is yet another example of this malady. In column after column, he continues to trot out the same tired, worn-out rhetoric on terrorism. Here is the gist of his biased view: the war in Iraq is *increasing* terrorism.

No, Muslim terrorists have been killing us for twenty-five years. Our government's leaders are being proactive in removing terror cells and avenging us for the civilian lives that were so ruthlessly snuffed out.

Hebert accuses our country of providing Al-Qaeda with a recruiting tool. News flash, Mr. Hebert! They don't need one. Terrorists are mindless killers who are motivated by hatred.

Hebert laments that other journalists can't see and won't report that which only he seems privy to. Hebert equates other news organizations' reluctance to repeat what he says as being irrelevant. Like O. J. Simpson's story. After all, we all know the media were just picking on O. J., right?

Mr. Hebert has ascertained that terrorism poses the greatest threat to America. Yes, externally. However, internally, from my vantage point as a concerned American and from personal experience, I see writers like Mr. Hebert as being the greatest threat to America. Why? Because it's from within our own borders.

Hebert continues to paint a gloomy picture of Iraq, making it seem as though anything we do will ultimately fail. Yet, and don't you love this, he proposes no solution of his own other than Hillary Clinton or Barak Obama, who would start planning new ways to surrender with dignity. Hebert downplays Iraq's acceptance of power as merely a ritual that has no substance. Most agree that we must have a starting point, and this is it.

Throughout Hebert's columns, the real reason for such vitriolic dissent always comes at the end, if you read between the lines: *Bush is insane for cutting taxes;* ***elect a Democrat.*** *Bush cannot win the war;* ***elect a Democrat.*** *Bush is a shameful president;* ***elect a Democrat.*** Ad nauseam.

But that kind of liberal bias is what America has come to expect from the *New York Times.* If you have lived in America for any substantial length of time and if you have read the *New York Times* or the *L.A. Times,* you might believe they are headquartered in China, North Korea, or Iran. They are agenda-driven to create a society that mirrors their own liberal bias. You see, they believe the rest of America is ignorant, uneducated, and uninformed if they don't line up like lemmings and follow them over the precipice to America's destruction.

You know, it has always been a hallmark of our nation for the media to remain neutral on every issue. Present the facts and then give the American people credit for having enough sense to make the correct decisions. That paradigm, by the way, accounts for Fox News's meteoric rise to success. But now this "liberal media bias madness" has so altered rational thinking that they actually believe they are qualified to think for the rest of us. That's scary!

The liberal media are fast removing freedom of intellectual choice from the American public. The arrogance displayed is appalling— that only they are somehow privileged to possess an insight that America does not or cannot have the capacity to understand. *So just believe what we say and do what we tell you.*

The effects of this shift in journalism and its new purpose are creating a climate that is forcing America to take sides against itself. We have experienced in history with the Civil War what that can do to a united nation. I have learned that biased media are driven by an insatiable appetite to create a society of their own design, without regard for others or what is best for America. The only thing that comes clearly into view is their own poisonous philosophy, and that drives them with a blind madness that transcends reason or consequence.

And what of those of us who oppose them? They show no tolerance for diversity of opinion. Yet when it pertains to liberal causes, they are all over the concept of tolerance; and the rest of America is branded as intolerant if we refuse to march lockstep as they pursue the biased agenda and lead America to ruin.

Unfortunately, this liberal media bias is spreading to small-town America and is no longer confined to large news outlets. In Columbia, South Carolina, the *State* newspaper, owned by McClatchy Co., champions itself as a paper representing all of South Carolina and the common good of all people. However, they cater to the liberal African American Left and openly extend guest-column status to radicals and NAACP mouthpieces, while refusing to print respectful rebuttals to articles steeped in racial prejudice toward whites and replete with lies.

The *State* editors offer a free pass time and again to black politicians. Almost every day there is a story of black injustice that occurred fifty years ago. Whites and other races are made to feel guilty by a continuous barrage of articles aimed at justifying reparations and affirmative action.

Employers and school districts are bullied into hiring incompetents. Law enforcement is mercilessly criticized for taking the only action available to them against blacks. Courts are blamed for convicting too many black males, yet South Carolina is plagued with an inordinate amount of black crime.

The *State* just doesn't get it. What difference should it make what race you are? If you break the law, you pay the penalty required by law.

South Carolina is suffering in the workplace and in its public schools because of this newspaper's relentless black agenda. Newspapers such as the *State* have swallowed the politically correct race-baited hook and have become biased in their coverage in order to punish what they perceive as a white culture that should be ashamed to be white.

People in South Carolina tell me they are becoming increasingly angry by this type of lopsided journalism. It keeps racial tensions in South Carolina at a fever pitch all the time, and the *State* won't let it die. Is that bias? Absolutely! But the editors would be righteously indignant at what I have said.

It gives concerned Americans an uneasy feeling to know just how much liberal bias is practiced in this country. It is one thing to be personally biased, but yet another to wrongly use your bias in a position of influence and trust. This does irreparable harm to the very nation that provides you that freedom and only asks of you to use it responsibly. Make a note; if the American public does not relegate this steady diet of liberal media bias to the trash heap, then liberal media madness cloaked as responsible journalism will undermine America's foundations of truth, and we will crumble and fall.

Chapter 9

Radical Islam

Terrorist Cult Cloaked in Religious Submission

—⁂—

R adical Islam is a terrorist cult. There, I've said it. No political correctness here. No bias or bigotry, only the truth. Though liberals will say I am an Islamophobe, that doesn't bother me. This is the truth that so many head-in-the sand people won't accept in the name of tolerance. Radical Islam is a terrorist cult. It is what they practice and what they believe, and they cloak it in religious submission. The word *Islam* means "submit" or "surrender." A Muslim is one who submits to Allah and confesses that Muhammad is his prophet.

America has always been a tolerant nation, and that grace has served us well until now. We have taken into the bosom of our nation people who will rip our country apart with violence. I have studied the Muslim doctrine from the Koran. Every devout Muslim feels that anybody who will not worship Allah should die. Any person who is not a Muslim is an infidel.

It is a fact that 50 percent of Muslims are fascists. Some like Al-Qaeda and Hamas try to carry out their radical beliefs by murderous terrorist attacks, while most, but not all, Muslims in America who publicly decry violence pray privately for our demise and that of every Jew. Jews are infidels to every Muslim, and Muslims pray thusly: "If a Jew hides behind a tree to avoid being seen and killed, that tree should fall on him and kill him." *[Koran]*

The Koran teaches that we must all convert to Islam or be slain and then suffer in hell. Only Muslims whose good deeds outweigh their sins or who die fighting non-Muslims will arrive in paradise with its sexual rewards.

I find it so interesting that the Koran never mentions their god as being a god of love. The Koran in Sura 3:79 says, "When you encounter the infidels, strike off their heads till ye have made a great slaughter among them, and the rest make fast in fetters [chains]."

As we have so painfully been made aware, these are cowards who delight in severing heads. We have allowed, through tolerance, seven million Muslims to live in America. We have gone so far as to embrace them and make excuses for their behavior.

I am reminded of the tale about a woman who found a poisonous snake that was freezing and could not move. The snake managed to say, "I'm so cold. Please pick me up and place me in your coat so that I may warm myself. I won't bite you." So the woman picked the snake up and placed him inside her coat.

After walking for a while, she suddenly felt a searing pain in her chest. She tore open her coat and discovered the snake had bitten her. She cried out in anguish, "You have bitten me! Now I will die."

The snake said, "You knew I was a poisonous snake when you took me into your bosom."

Let's bring that home. We know that radical Islam is a terrorist, murderous cult, a twisted religion that mutilates, beats, oppresses, and kills its women. It bombs, slaughters, and executes innocent people in hospitals, shopping malls, homes, school buses, restaurants, and anywhere else where it can find a helpless or unsuspecting victim. It straps explosive devices to children and teens who unknowingly blow themselves up and the innocent with them.

Radical Muslims are driven by their allegiance to the Koran and their god, Allah and his prophet Muhammad. History tells us that Muhammad was born in the city of Mecca around the year 570. He was orphaned and worked in camel caravans as an adult. Over the course of his troubled life, he owned ten wives, one of which was nine years old.

Khadijah, the rich widow, afforded him the opportunity to spend more time immersed in his religion after he claimed that Allah sent the angel Gabriel to tell him that he would be the sole prophet of Allah. When the people rebelled against him, his followers were led by Muhammad to start a cleansing war, killing those who opposed him. He defeated Mecca. He destroyed all the other idols of worship and replaced them with a dark stone to which every Muslim must bow. He murdered every opponent, and men who were taken in battle were killed when they would not worship Muhammad and his god. The captives' wives and children were sold as slaves to traveling caravans. Thus radical Islam was born.

Muhammad took armies of Muslims and went into cities and villages, and if the people there did not convert to Islam, they were killed. Some were impaled on poles outside the city. Pregnant women were disemboweled and put on poles with their dead babies exposed as an example of the horror that awaited anyone who would not convert to radical Islam.

King Louis VII and King Conrad III sent armies of crusaders to stop Islam's murderous attacks on innocent people.[*Wikipedia*] That holy war between Christianity and Islam is a driving force today. The holy jihad is a continuation of that war. In Sudan, over a million people have been slaughtered simply for being Christians. It's interesting that the people in Mecca discovered and said that Muhammad was a madman.

Muhammad's violence and bloodshed continued as he soon learned from his victories in Medina that the fear of dying was the way to build Islam. In Mecca he failed to persuade people to convert to Islam just through teaching doctrine. Intimidation and murder turned out to be the effective methods of choice.

Since that time until now, it has been the practice of Muslim nations to persecute Christians and Jews simply because of their faith. These governments not only look the other way when Christians in Muslim countries are jailed, tortured, and killed, but they endorse it; and that's a fact!

America has never had a more deadly enemy than radical Islam. The freedom of our nation and our national security depend on how we choose to deal with this growing threat. Whether we honestly recognize it or whether we stay in denial and hope for the best, the best will not come. The dangerous precedent that is being set in America is this: if a national leader speaks out against radical Islam, more Americans are then killed in foreign countries. The sudden rush to judgment by irresponsible politicians and the liberal media says that the responsibility of more deaths lies with the man or woman who has the integrity and courage to denounce violent terrorist acts and those responsible, but not with the killers themselves. How irresponsible is that!

We as Americans can no longer tap dance around this growing threat. We cannot allow ourselves to be intimidated into silent oblivion or held captive by the ignorant theory that speaking out will make matters worse. Matters are worse! Remember, these lunatics don't ever need a reason to kill; they have it! The question that almost everyone asks is, Why? Why this burning maniacal hatred for Jews and Americans? The answer is both simple and surprising. Yet those who know the answer want to look elsewhere. But here it is: they hate our God—the God of heaven; the God of the Bible; the God of Abraham, Isaac, and Jacob; the God of the Jews; the God of Christians; the God of America.

Let me explain. In Genesis 16:1–12, Sarah wants a child, but she is barren. God promises Abraham an heir, but Sarah refuses to wait on God, so she asks Abraham to take Hagar, her Egyptian handmaid, and father a child by her for Sarah. After Hagar becomes pregnant, she begins to mock Sarah.

In verse 9, God told Hagar to submit herself under the hand of Sarah. Then it was told Hagar that she would bear a son. His name would be Ishmael. But in verse 12, it was prophesied that Ishmael would be a wild man. His hand would be against every man, and every man's hand would be against him. He would dwell in the presence of his brethren, the Hebrews (Jews). So this son of a Hebrew and an Egyptian would be an Arab.

The word *wild* means unreasonable. You cannot find anybody on Earth today more unreasonable than Ishmael's descendants. Look at the events today. Every nation is fighting terrorism. Prophecy is being fulfilled.

In Genesis 17:16–19, God tells Abraham that Sarah will bear a child and call him Isaac. Abraham laughs and says, "A ninety-year-old woman having a child?" Then in verse 18, Abraham says, "Let Ishmael be the heir of the covenant," but God rejected that suggestion.

In verse 19, God tells Abraham that Sarah will have a boy. His name will be Isaac, and the everlasting covenant will be with Isaac, not Ishmael. God says in verse 20 that Ishmael will multiply and prosper (oil).

By Genesis 21:1–21, Isaac has been born, and Ishmael begins to despise him and torment him. In verse 10, Sarah tells Abraham to send Hagar and Ishmael away, because she knows Isaac is Abraham's sole heir and the recipient of God's covenant.

Abraham sent Hagar and Ishmael away. God protected Hagar and Ishmael because Ishmael was of Abraham, but Ishmael was rejected as the heir of God's covenant. In Genesis 22:2, God referred to Isaac as Abraham's only son and did not recognize Ishmael as a son of the covenant.

Muhammad became prominent in the Arab lands in the seventh century. The Old Testament chronicles of the Jews were approximately two thousand years old. Abraham was considered the father of the Jews, and Moses was the lawgiver (Ten Commandments). Then Jesus came on the scene, and Christianity was born. Christianity had been growing for approximately 550 years.   M u h a m m a d was initially a merchant trading goods throughout the region. In creating Islam, Muhammad lifted accounts from the Old Testament and the New Testament and began to formulate a new religion, one that would also incorporate the false gods of that day. Muhammad also claimed to have received a special vision and divine guidance from Allah.

Now remember, Muhammad was a descendant of Ishmael and Hagar. Hagar was an Egyptian. She came from a culture that worshipped over five hundred false gods. In Muhammad's day, the Arab nations bowed to over three hundred false gods. The god that Muhammad worshipped was Allah. Allah historically was Al-ilah, the moon god of the Quarish tribe of Arabia. Muhammad elevated Al-ilah to Allah. He set about to deny and destroy the other three hundred gods of Arabia.

History tells us that at the onset a wife was created for Allah. Her name was Allat. Together they represented the worship of the sun and the moon. Muhammad claimed that of all the gods in the Arab nations, only Allah was the true god, and he alone was Allah's prophet. He set himself up as the promised seed of Allah. He perverted Old Testament Scripture by claiming it was Ishmael, not Isaac who was the heir of the covenant.

In order to establish a divine lineage, Muhammad had to prove, though falsely, that Ishmael was the father of all living and had inherited the covenant. He further perverted the biblical lineage of both King David and Jesus and pronounced them to be prophets of Allah, thereby making them from the lineage of Ishmael. The Jewish people were outraged that Holy Scripture was being perverted in such a way and that their covenant with almighty God was being robbed from them, at least in the Koran. When Muhammad encoun- tered the Jewish resistance to the Koran and this new Islamic reli- gion, he began to burn with a hatred for Jews, much like Ishmael did for Isaac.

History tells us that Muhammad was incensed that God had not chosen Ishmael as the heir. After all, he was the firstborn. That was a grievous insult. He was further angered when he discovered that Hagar and Ishmael were banished because it was obvious that the

162

Hebrews and an Arab were never going to get along. Muhammad began to seethe with a great hatred for the Jews, and he began to personally hate this God who had acted in such a way.

Thus radical Islam was born, a religion based on revenge and predicated upon a god of death instead of a God of grace. When God sent Jesus to die for the world's sins, thus connecting the Jews and Christians, the Muslims discovered a new group of people to hate. The Jews worshipped not the same Savior as the Christians, but the same God.

To this very day every Muslim hates every Jew. Muslims will not live in peace with Jews any more than Ishmael would with Isaac. The Muslim nations want to annihilate Israel and any nation who dares support her.

Now, you will hear others give a different take on the unrest in the Middle East. This account I have given is the truth. To ignore it, you have to ignore history, ignore the facts, and ignore the actions and the evidence. To simply lie about it is just for political correctness.   Colleges and high schools are teaching students not to blame the hijackers for September 11, but to blame Americans' intolerance instead, advancing the thought that if we are more tolerant and cooperative, terrorists will not hate us. We just need to negotiate with them with more sensitivity.

The University of North Carolina is requiring incoming students to read *Approaching the Qur'an,* a book that spins the Koran to make it less threatening and more palatable to whet the appetites of gullible idiots. *World Net Daily* reported about a pamphlet that calls Muslims to kill Westerners and Christians. It is being distributed in Pakistan. Here is what it says: "The nonbelievers have made the lives of Muslims miserable, leaving them with no option except jihad. It is the supreme duty of Muslims to trace out Americans, Israelis, and Westerners. Whether they are army men or not and kill them, whether they are in the city, air, sea, or desert." Every Muslim everywhere is instructed not to work with Christians or make contact with them because they are the enemies of Islam.

Islamic fascists exploded car bombs outside five targeted churches in Iraq, claiming this was in retaliation for the Christian Crusades. (As I mentioned in this chapter, the crusaders were armies sent to stop militant Muslims from mass murder.) The attacks on the churches in Iraq killed eleven people. Others staggered into the streets, screaming in terror and bleeding profusely. The churches were engulfed in flames and destroyed.

For a long period, the Christian churches have been left alone to worship, but Islam is turning up the heat. In one church in Mosul, worshippers were finishing their prayers and leaving when rocket-propelled grenades were fired into the church.

The attacks against Christians are escalating. In January a bus loaded with Christian women on the way to work at a U.S. military base was attacked by hooded thugs who wantonly killed the women. As you can tell from these accounts, these are heartless devils who are also cowards. If strong action is not taken in this country, the violence against Americans and Christians in the Middle East will come to America.

Am I right? Well, consider this: Two mosque leaders were arrested in Albany, New York. They were trying to buy a grenade launcher. Are we listening? Are we paying attention? Once the majority of people in this country are Islamic, it will be forced upon the rest of us, or we will be put to death. Can it happen? All we need to do is pretend it won't.

Imagine the blast of a ship's horn sounding in your neighborhood three times a day. What a nerve-wracking experience that would be! Residents in Dearborn, Michigan are forced to listen to something just as unsettling. Area mosques are allowed by the city council to broadcast Islamic calls to prayer over loudspeakers. There is still an ongoing battle over this blatant intrusion by Muslims.

Islam is fast converting every inmate it can in every prison in America. In other countries where Muslims have taken over, they have freed violent criminals and let them loose on an unsuspecting populace. Why would they do such a thing? These inmates were Muslims.

Ibrahim Hopper, director of communications for the Council of American Islamic Relations, stated, *"I would like the government of the United States to be Islamic in the future."* This should be a wake-up call to every American. This is a statement of the clear intent of this violent cult.   The threat this scenario poses has to be frightening to even the most optimistic and brave among us. We cannot allow ourselves to be taken in by soft rhetoric or be intimidated by the words *bigot* and *intolerance*. Why? Because we are not afforded the luxury of being tolerant with radical Islam. If we as Americans buy into this new thinking—that we should accept something that is this harmful to our religious practice, democracy, freedom and security—then we as a people will suffer the horrible consequences of our own weakness and naïveté.

Just how naïve are we? Just how deep are radical Islamists entrenched in America? American Congress for Truth, a watchdog organization that informs the public of dangerous Muslim activity in America, had the following on their website on March 17, 2007, from *Investors Business Daily:*

Homeland Security: Authorities across the pond now fear that even more Muslims, possibly numbering in the thousands, are plotting terror. On this end, however, U.S. officials still can't see anything in the pipeline.

Either the British have better intelligence than we do, or we don't have any radicalized Muslim communities here in America. Sanguine U.S. authorities are guessing the latter.

Responding to new alarms raised by the Brits, Homeland Security Secretary Michael Chertoff says not to worry; the threat inside America is less severe. He maintains that this country doesn't have the kind of "pockets" of concentrated radicals seen in Britain, where terrorists can find support and plot with virtual impunity. Chertoff must not get out much.

Right across the Potomac from his office is the second-highest concentration of Muslims in the country. Bailey's Crossroads, Virginia, is teeming with Islamic radicals just as hostile to the U.S. government as their counterparts in London.

Bailey's Crossroads is the heart of the Wahhabi Corridor, which includes the safe houses where the hijackers stayed and the mosque where they and dozens of other terrorists have worshipped.

Another area mosque preached to members of the Virginia Jihad Network, who plotted to kill American soldiers after 9/11 and praised the space shuttle *Columbia* disaster as a "good omen" for Islam.

The area also includes two luxury apartment high-rises that erupted into cheers when the World Trade

Center fell on 9/11. Law enforcement has dubbed them the "Taliban Towers." Investigators routinely find posters and computer screen savers celebrating Osama bin Laden as a hero.

Down the street is a Saudi charitable front for Al-Qaeda once run by bin Laden's nephew. The I.S. branch of the dangerous Muslim Brotherhood is in the same office park. Farther down in Alexandria is the Saudi madrassa that's graduated several terrorists, including the Al-Qaeda operative who plotted to assassinate President Bush.

Agents on the ground working the inordinate number of terror cases in the area say it's no less than the base of operations for the bad guys in America—and its right in Chertoff's backyard. Despite raid after raid, however, none of the entities along the Wahhabi Corridor has been shut down. Thanks to institutionalized political correctness and Saudi Embassy complaints, the terror-supporting infrastructure has not been dismantled. The Brits turned a blind eye to radicalism in their backyard, but no more. They're finally cracking down.

We haven't learned our lesson for some odd reason. To suddenly decree this side of the pond a radical-free zone after what happened here just over five years ago is fatuous. The hijackers didn't operate in isolation, like visitors from outer space. They were secreted inside the Muslim community for well over a year and got substantial aid and comfort from dozens of facilitators at no less than seven mosques from coast to coast. Some knew the evil they planned and helped them anyway.

Assimilation? Hardly. In Bailey's Crossroads, skinned goats are delivered daily to several halal butcher shops located in shopping centers where all the signs are in Arabic. Women shop in head-to-toe black abayas. You'd never know this is a suburb of the nation's capital. Concerned long-time residents have seen it turn into "Northern Virginiastan."

The pundits who mouth pleasant platitudes about American Muslims being more "integrated" have never spent much time in northern Virginia, or for that matter, in Bridgeview, Illinois; or Jersey City, New Jersey;

or Dearborn, Michigan, where residents are routinely subjected to rallies and marches for Hezbollah and other terror groups.

These places look and sound more like little Cairo than any American city, and they provide perfect cover for Muslim terrorists and their supporters. Terror experts say there are hundreds if not thousands of potential suicide bombers already established inside the Muslim communities in America. They need to be ferreted out.

The Muslim religion is diametrically opposed to everything America was founded on — all the wonderful ideals we have embraced that have served us so well. The doctrine of radical Islam flies in the face of the doctrine of the loving God America was founded on — the God who has richly blessed America and the God who has kept us free, the God who has guided us to persevere through Hitler's hell and who teaches us to love other people, to worship in peace and harmony, and to live together as neighbors and countrymen.

There must never be any room in America for a religious doctrine that so perverts the minds of its followers that they turn into rabid, unthinking animals who do not possess even one virtue of a human being. This doctrine teaches the hedonistic philosophy of the afterlife, that physical pleasure is the highest good and that the highest pleasure can be obtained through violence. Quoting from the Koran. "By the mercy of Allah, no talking in heaven by leaders, only virgins with large bosoms and soft eyes. Each honored male will be rewarded with seventy-two virgins and they shall never grow old, and the euphoria shall never end."

How did we ever arrive at the state we are presently experiencing in America? We seem to be passively accepting our fate rather than rattling the sabers. What has happened to us? We don't seem to possess the fight to stand against evil no matter what form it comes in, whether military aggression or religious lunacy.

If we continue to believe the carefully constructed lies about radical Islam from the politically correct crowd and if we continue to yield to societal pressures to accept that which has America's death written all over it, then the days, weeks, months, and years ahead will be the most horrific we have ever experienced as a free nation. We will live a national nightmare. If the majority of Americans cannot and will not acknowledge the threat of radical Islam, then they will ensure our deaths.

I am beginning to wonder if there are peaceful Muslims or only plotting Muslims. Peaceful Muslims must stand up, be heard, and be counted, if they indeed are peaceful. They must condemn the bloodthirsty lunatics of their religion. Recently I asked an imam if he would condemn terrorists who claim to be his brothers and if he would say they were doing an evil work that has nothing to do with any *living God*. He said, "No I won't." There it is!

After the bombings that killed fifty people in London, CAIR (Council of American Islamic Relations) gave lip service to the incident, mildly speaking out. But a close hearing revealed that they didn't say anything with very much conviction.

When the plot to blow up Transatlantic Airlines was unveiled, Muslim leaders in Britain and CAIR in the United States blamed British and American foreign policy, calling them the real terrorists. Imagine that. CAIR went a step further by publicly criticizing President Bush for using the term *Islamic fascists* to describe terrorists. President Bush was hoping to draw a distinction between wanton killers and Muslims who should enjoy democracy in a freedom-loving nation.

Debra Saunders, a columnist for *Creators Syndicate*, wrote this about Daveed Gartenstein-Ross:

> Fascinating memoir that came out in February 2007: "My Year Inside Radical Islam" Gartenstein-Ross describes that he was drawn to Islam because he saw it as a religion of peace. Over time, however, he watched himself and those around him seduced into a fanaticism that required them to loathe not only non-Muslims, but also Muslims who belonged to the wrong sect, listened to music, or shaved. He had expected an open, accepting religion, only to hear sheikhs arguing that it is acceptable to kill civilians for jihad and that good Muslims should work to replace democratic government with sharia law. The hate chased Gartenstein-Ross from Islam, but only after it sucked him into believing that unacceptable actions were holy.

Daveed Ross discovered what those of us who know Islam have known for a very long time.

Worse than that are radical Muslims who meet in mosques on American soil and cheer when another mall explosion kills more innocent people. Then they kneel and pray. Pray for what? That radical Islam will take over the United States, that's what!

Now, this may shake you, but it underscores my point about the "peaceful mosques" in this country. U.S. mosques have played host to fundraising banquets. Some of the participants were being indicted by the federal government. During these so-called charity events, skits, role-playing, and poems made into songs were performed. Sounds innocent enough, right? But all the entertainment had one central theme: the destruction of Israel and her people. The indictments further stated that these activities championed the nobility of killing Jews any way they could.

Radical Islamics worked to elect Cynthia McKinney to Congress. McKinney is known to be sympathetic to the cause of Islam and would have been dangerous if she had been elected. Thankfully, she was defeated. Her press conference after her defeat was a mob scene of angry Muslims.

Unfortunately, Keith (Hakim Mohammad) Ellison of Minnesota was the first-ever Muslim politician to be elected to serve in the U.S. Congress. Upon being elected, he promptly said that he would not take the oath of office on the Bible but only on the Koran, and the U.S. Congress was too spineless to stop him. After his election, Ellison did not talk about his plans to serve his country or how to solve the problems of government. He was more concerned about his in-your-face statement. Why? Because it was foremost in his mind, and he could not resist expressing his disrespect for the Bible.

Muslim doctrine, though, is clear; a Muslim cannot swear allegiance to the U.S Constitution and also have a devout belief in Allah. Even Muslims will agree with that. So where does that leave his constituents? It leaves them with a Muslim who disrespects the Constitution of the United States in favor of Muslim law.

The traditional oath on the Holy Bible signified that the person being sworn in would support and defend the Constitution above all others. But you must understand. Islam rejects the God of America in favor of Allah. Will Ellison do what is best for America? No, he won't. He will do that which will aid the spread of radical Islam.

Judge Roy Moore in his communiqué reported that: "Jafir Sheikh Idris, founder and chairman of American Open University, a radical Islamic school that in the past has received funds from suspected Al-Qaeda sources and who supports Islamic law, stated that 'Islam cannot be separated from the state,' and that no Muslim elected to Congress or the White House (they have designs on that office) can swear to uphold the United States Constitution and still be a Muslim, because the laws of Allah as expressed in the Koran are supreme. Idris was recently deported for his illegal activities but he is well-versed in Islam's guidebook."

According to a December 6, 2006, *World Net Daily Article*, "Keith Ellison's campaign was not only backed by the Council of American Islamic Relations, which shapes the views of American Open University, but he also spoke on the same program as American Open leaders." Is the *true* picture of Ellison starting to come into focus?

Bob Unruh writing in *World Net Daily* countered Hakim Mohammad's misleading statement that Thomas Jefferson's owner-ship of a Koran meant that he somehow endorsed it. Hakim went so far as to borrow Jefferson's copy from the Library of Congress for his swearing in. He claimed that Jefferson's owning a copy proved it was a historical document in our national history and demonstrated that Jefferson was a broad visionary thinker who not only possessed a Koran but enjoyed reading it.

Thomas Jefferson read it all right, but for an entirely different reason than stated by Hakim Ellison. Unruh quoted the publisher of the *U.S. Veteran Dispatch,* Ted Sampley, as saying, "At the time Jefferson owned the book, he needed to know everything possible about Muslims because he was about to advocate war against the Islamic Barbary states of Morocco, Algeria, Tunisia, and Tripoli."

Sampley further states that "for 1,000 years Muslim pirates had cruised the African and Mediterranean coastline, pillaging villages and abducting slaves, mostly by making predawn raids that left high casualty rates." It was typical of Muslim raiders to kill off as many of the non-Muslim older men and women as possible so the preferred take of only young women could be collected, noting that the latter "were sought for their value as concubines in Islamic markets," while boys, as young as nine or ten years old, were often mutilated to create eunuchs who would bring higher prices in the slave markets of the Middle East.

In 1784 Thomas Jefferson, John Adams, and Benjamin Franklin were commissioned by Congress to find a solution for this ever-growing Muslim threat. Adams wanted to take the coward's way out and pay off the Muslim pirates. But Thomas Jefferson stood firm and boldly declared that a military solution was the only answer. *War!*

After meeting with the Muslim ambassador, the three men gave this account to Congress: Islam was founded on the laws of their prophet, and it was written in the Koran that any nation that would not yield to Muslim law was an infidel. It was the Muslims' holy calling to fight and kill infidels anywhere they were encountered. Their book gave Muslims the supreme authority to imprison, maim, torture, behead, and enslave anybody who resisted, all in the name of Allah.

The United States government unwisely paid millions in such ransom (and you can believe that modern-day Muslims know their history) until Jefferson was elected president of the United States. Jefferson immediately sent the *U.S.S. Constellation* and six other ships of war to the Mediterranean Sea. That is when America entered the Barbary Wars.

Gary De Mar, president of AmericanVision.org quotes from Joseph Wheelan's excellent book, *Jefferson's War: America's First*

War on Terror: "Too long, for the honor of nations have those barbarians been allowed to trample on the sacred faith of treaties, on the rights and laws of human nature!" Jefferson's war pitted a modern republic with a medieval autocracy whose credo was piracy and terror. It matched an ostensibly Christian nation against an avowed Islamic one that professed to despise Christians.

Here is what Joseph Wheelan determined that Jefferson learned from the Koran: Unless a nation submitted to Islam, whether that nation was the initial aggressor or not, that nation was by definition at war with Islam. That is why Jefferson studied the Koran. He knew that if Americans ever capitulated (as we are doing now), Muslims would overrun America. Keith (Hakim Mohammad) Ellison is simply a liar—and history proves it—when he tries to imply that Thomas Jefferson embraced the Koran as anything other than the guidebook for terror.

World Net Daily further stated that Keith Ellison Mohammad has admitted, with no contrition, to making anti-Jewish and anti-Christian statements. At his political rallies, he allowed his supporters to shout *Allahu Akbar.* This was the same phrase allegedly used by Muhammad Atta and the other suicide pilots on 9/11. Suicide bombers scream this statement before blowing up themselves and other innocent people. Muslim executioners shout it when severing heads.

Hakim Muhammad has spoken to Islamic groups, but he has avoided *World Net Daily's* simple question: will you base your decisions as a congressman on the laws of the United States of America and its binding Constitution or on the Koran? But true to Muslim form, he said, "My faith informs these things."

World Net Daily has courageously reported that "Hakim Muhammad holds to a radical school of thought that requires absolute loyalty to the Koran over the U.S. Constitution." As Robert Sumner so aptly said, "Are we disturbed? We had better be!"

Numerous reports of June 17, 2004, described the intent of Muslim members of the University of California Irvine's graduation class to wear green sashes that had the word *shada* boldly printed in Arabic. These sashes were to be worn along with the commencement robes. Because the word *shada* is an inducement to carry out violence, these Muslim students should never have been allowed to wear them.

Shada is a word primarily used to mean "martyrdom." This type of martyrdom can be achieved only by people who are suicide bombers. Most Jews who are familiar with the term know it means "kill the Jews." Yet, the California Irvine administration did nothing to stop it, nor did they stop the anti-Jewish meetings that were held on campus during the year by the Muslim Student Union.

Many other students at the university openly say this organization is a front for terrorist activity. Columnist Arnold Steinberg, writing in *Front Page,* unequivocally stated that Muslim students at U.C. Irvine support Hamas, who are known Middle East terrorists. The Muslim Student Union placed posters on campus that compared the Star of David to the German swastika. Guest speakers invited to U.C. Irvine by this Muslim group routinely urged students to begin an Islamic revolution in America, following the lead of Hamas in its war against Jews and Americans. Jews, protesting the hate speeches of these soon-to-be Muslim terrorists, were unsuccessful in getting the U.C. Irvine administration to do anything about it. As always, they cited First Amendment rights.

I can assure you, the framers of our constitution never meant for freedom to extend to a violent cult that seeks to overthrow America and kill her people. That is outrageously ludicrous. I'll go ahead and say it: U.C. Irvine is run by a bunch of fools.

Is the picture beginning to come into focus? Are we seeing clearly what is happening? Do we possess the vision to predict where all of this is going if we don't come to our collective senses?

The followers of Muhammad have been estimated to be more than one billion people. All Muslims are not Arabs. Islam is not confined to a nationality. At the last research count, Islam dominates at least fifty nations whose sole purpose and goal is to control other nations for Allah.

The Islamic system of sharia law has destroyed every nation and province that it has conquered. The supposed supremacy of Islam has been deeply branded into the consciences of Muslims, and there can be room for no other. A new law presented to Pakistan's governing body calls for the death sentence to be imposed on any man who leaves Islam and life in prison for any woman. How's that for tolerance?

Here in America the double standard is prevalent. Muslims are provided freedom and protection to worship and spread their religion. This religion holds a hatred for Jews and Christians. Some politicians will make you literally sick with their fawning over the Muslim vote.

Muslims routinely issue press releases griping about perceived insults to Islam, using words such as *prejudice, intolerance,* and *hatred.* I would challenge every American to get on the Internet and pull up a Muslim website and listen to an imam spew his hatred toward Christians and Christianity, mocking Jesus and ridiculing the Bible.

Excuse me! And *they* have the audacity to use words such as *hate* and *discrimination.*

In Muslim countries, converts to Christianity often suffer death, or beatings and maiming. Freedom of religion is unheard of. America must be educated as to how Islam is really working in our nation. This is a strong statement, but, I believe, in the case of Islam, a true and needed one.

America has become *too free* when we offer sanctuary and unre-stricted license to people who practice a religion that calls for the annihilation of two entire nations of people, America and Israel. We have defeated so many enemies who sought our death. How is it that we have become so disinterested at this point in history that we would allow this to happen?

I'll tell you how! We have become reluctant to present and then stand up and defend the *truth.* We have drunk the elixir of pacifism, and that will spell our doom. We cannot allow ourselves to become a people who opt to ignore an advancing evil rather than confront it and be called religious bigots.

We must remind ourselves that if what we say about Islam is true—and it is—then we are not bigots of any sort. For the survival of our way of life and for our national security, we must not allow fear to dominate our actions, because that is exactly what radical Islam is counting on in its bid to take over America.

Muslims at this point are still a weak minority in the United States. But they are striving to become the majority, if only by protests. Some will continue to appear to be friendly and peace-loving, exchanging all the niceties that you would expect from a peace-seeking people. But, make no mistake. As their numbers grow and their hold on power increases, they will begin to agitate for rights. Led by the Council on American Islamic Relations (CAIR), Muslims are becoming bolder.

Let me illustrate. After praying at the boarding gate, Muslim imams boarded a U.S. Airways flight bound for Phoenix, Arizona, and they immediately began to exhibit bizarre behavior that unnerved passengers and crew. They requested seat belt extensions and were loudly conversing with each other in Arabic. Passengers feared that the seat belts might be used as weapons, so they reported the imans.

The imams' unsettling behavior led to their expulsion from the plane by U.S. Airway officials. The imams indignantly rushed to a waiting press conference. The media had been called even before the incident happened. The imams had planned the charade and baited other passengers and airline personnel. You guessed it! It was an old fashioned setup.

But it didn't stop with the press conference. The imams filed a lawsuit against the airline, even extending the suit to include the reporting passengers and claiming—now get this—the passengers were looking for an opportunity to discriminate against them because of their national origin and religion. What a crock! *[The State News]*

But you can see the plan unfold: *We are going to fake you out and intimidate you so that when we really are attempting to take over a plane, you will be too scared to say anything for fear of being sued; and the airline will ignore our actions until we have slit throats and accomplished our mission.* That's how the plan will work if left unchallenged.

Where was the Council on American Islamic Relations in all this? Did they care about relations with Americans? No! They backed the lawsuit, and truth be known, they probably had a hand in the deed.

Attorneys representing Muslims will now seek to punish anybody who dares question Muslim behavior. There are further disturbing instances of a growing agitation. Recent clamoring by Muslims for footbaths in airports and universities has caused angst among officials. The University of Michigan at Dearborn recently caved in to agitation, approving two footbaths in unisex bathrooms.

These types of stupid, pinhead decisions show a blatant favoritism for Islam over other religions. But they want us to favor them so they can claim America as their own. If this ever happens, our religious rights and practices will be trampled upon. We have to wise up!

Under the rule of Islam, whether a nation is converted to it or not, those people will be its slaves. This follows the practice of Muslims over the centuries to conquer and exact submission by military conquest. After Muslim pressure, Carver Elementary School in San Diego, California, altered its recess schedule to accommodate Muslim students. Parents ought to be outraged that their children must bow to the whim of Islam while ignoring the freedom of Christian children to pray.

How far will Muslims go to indoctrinate our children to the Muslim religion and lifestyle? How far will stupid, spineless school administrators go to appease Muslims? Are there any dangerous precedents? You better believe it!

Agape Press reported the following:

A federal appeals court is being asked to reconsider its ruling that allows public schools to teach junior high students how to "become Muslims." The Thomas More Law Center, a national public-interest law firm based in Ann Arbor, Michigan, is asking the entire Ninth U.S. Circuit Court of Appeals to rule on what can be done in public schools with regard to teaching Islam and other religions.

Several parents sued California's Byron Union School District for requiring their seventh-grade children to participate in a three-week class activity in which they not only had to study important Islamic figures and wear traditional Muslim attire, but were also required to observe the "five pillars" of the Islamic faith, adopt Muslim names, recite a portion of a Muslim prayer, and even stage their own jihad, or "holy war." The plaintiffs' attorney, the Thomas More Law Center's Ed White, believes the school district violated the parents' and children's constitutional rights to free exercise of religion.

Earlier, White had asked a three-judge panel of the Ninth Circuit to overturn a previous San Francisco federal district court's ruling that the Byron Union School District did not violate the U.S. Constitution. However, the Ninth Circuit panel of judges upheld the lower court's determination in a brief, unpublished memorandum decision. . . .

White says the Byron Union School District never informed the parents about an exercise that would be grading their children on how well they observed the tenets of Islam. In fact, he points out, "The parents were never told that there was even a way to opt their child out of such an activity."

Actually, the only way the parents found out about the school's Islamic exercise, the attorney points out, was virtually by accident. He says a Byron Union District mom was "looking through her son's book bag and asked, 'Hey, what's all this stuff?' and the kid said, 'Oh, we're doing this in school now.' So the parents objected, but it was after the class (activity) was over."

So it was after the fact that parents learned how, for three weeks in 2001, their children were told they would "become Muslims" and had worn identification tags bearing their new Muslim names along with the star and crescent moon symbols of Islam. The children received materials telling them to "remember Allah always so that you may prosper," and they made banners to hang in their classroom, inscribing them with the *Basmala,* a phrase from the Koran used in Muslim prayers that is translated, "in the name of Allah, the Merciful, the Compassionate."

Richard Thomas, chief counsel of the Thomas More Law Center, commented that if students had been instructed on Christianity in the same manner as they were on Islam in this case, the court would most likely have found a constitutional violation.

Ed White agrees. The parents' lawyer says the courts should not be allowing this apparent double standard on the teaching of religion in public schools.

I have a message for Muslims: if you enroll your kids in a public school in America, then you have to adapt—not the other way around.

When my sons were young, they each received a piggy bank from the bank that we used. They had fun saving coins, and it was exciting for them. Now a number of banks have discontinued the practice of handing out piggy banks to children. Why? *Political correctness.* Some banks were informed by local Muslims that piggy banks would offend Muslims because they were caricatures of swine.

Who the heck cares if Muslims are offended? They read offense into everything American, and if allowed, they will agitate and make everything we do as Americans offensive to them. Well, millions of Americans and I are fed up with this junk, and we say if they are offended by our culture and practices, then they can go back to their sand dunes. If they don't, then one of these days, Americans are going to get a belly full of their religious nit-picking.

Amazingly, after posturing over a piggy bank, Islamic militants see no problem with using a likeness of Mickey Mouse on Al-Qsa television (operated by Hamas thugs) to brainwash children into taking over hated Israel for Allah.

We as Americans must make it crystal clear that we will not be pushed around in our own nation. Muslims can either learn to adapt to the hospitality and laws of a civilized and respectful society or leave. It is that simple. This insanity must stop now!

We are at war with rabid Muslims, and they are at war with us. All one had to do was watch the news reports from around the world after September 11 to see millions of Muslims dancing in the streets, shouting and burning the American flag. Seven million were in our own nation, living among us, worshipping their god and his prophet, biding their time to strike us. Yet in a Muslim-controlled country, a Christian or an American dare not give out a piece of literature or meet together for fear of instant imprisonment, maiming, or death.

Is Islam tolerant or fair? You be the judge. But I personally don't believe they are, and they have proved it. What will it take? How many thousands of Americans must die in order for us to truly understand and believe that the followers of Muhammad see themselves as creating a world that is totally Islamic and enslaving every nation on Earth?

Sura 4:74 and 76 in the Koran says, "Let those who would exchange the life of this world for the hereafter fight for the cause of Allah; whether they die or conquer, we shall richly reward them. . . . The true believers fight for the cause of Allah, but the infidels (Jews and Christians) fight for their idols. Fight then against the priests of Satan." This is what Muslims believe and what they practice. Islam means "submission." The one submitting is called a Muslim. Make no mistake; a true Muslim will submit to whatever it takes to further the cause of Islam.

Even those Muslims who appear to be doing good cannot be trusted. For example, the Holy Land Foundation for Relief and

Development based in Richardson, Texas, and set up in other locations in Jerusalem, New Jersey, Illinois, and California, is a tax-exempt organization and the largest Muslim charity in America. The leaders have been indicted by the federal government for funneling millions of dollars to Hamas, the terror arm of Palestine. Hamas has been responsible for numerous suicide bomb attacks in Israel. The money this group raised came from trusting Americans who believed they were giving to starving families, orphanages, schools, and hospitals.

Then U.S. Attorney General John Ashcroft said in newspapers"Holy Land had operated illegally and had funneled approximately twelve million dollars to Hamas since 1995." The indictments charged the conspirators with providing material support for a foreign terrorist organization, conspiracy, money laundering, and filing false tax statements to the I.R.S. It is also interesting that two of the co-conspirators are in other countries and are on an ongoing fugitive list. The indictment accuses Holy Land operatives of meeting with Hamas as early as 1993, when they first plotted to financially support Hamas and cloak the true intents from the public. Can we trust Islam? No! Not now, not ever!

Islam has a carefully laid out plan to defeat the will of America, to destroy the U.S. military, and to occupy our government. We erred when we allowed a Muslim state to ever be established inside of our nation, and now we are compelled to stop the advancement and undo the damage that has already been done.

Fighting for America has never been for the squeamish or assigned to those who have not the resolve to value what America is and represents. We are in a war! To some it is now a cliché, but we had better not forget 9/11. Radical Islamists will not, and if there is a new terror attack, millions may die.

I am convinced that the future of our children and grandchildren hangs in the balance. If you do not believe that Islam is the greatest threat ever to America's freedom, then please prepare your children and grandchildren to live in a country controlled by wild-eyed imams who use sharia law to crush any dissent.

Radical Islam is a terrorist cult cloaked in religious submission and worship, an evil that America cannot ignore.

Chapter 10

Financial Seduction

Cloaked as Legalized Gambling

—꿍—

When I was young, a high school teacher told our class, "A man who gambles and wins is a thief, and a man who gambles and loses is a fool." Growing up, I never forgot that statement.

The first time I saved enough money to attend the state fair, my grandmother said, "Son, do not gamble. You can't beat those men at their own game. They will take all of your money." I never forgot my grandmother's wise counsel either.

There is never any confidence placed in gambling, just chance and unnecessary risk. Gambling has been defined this way: accepting a careless risk and hoping for a bountiful gain far above what was initially invested.

I never knew but one man who bettered his immediate situation by gambling. He traveled to Las Vegas in a $35,000 Lincoln Continental, and he rode a $150,000 Greyhound bus back home!

Gambling robs a man or woman of reason. Caution is thrown to the wind by an addictive desire and a cheap thrill to get something for nothing. Gambling produces no personal growth, accomplishes no social good. Gambling is taking a chance, somehow believing you will beat the odds and be the lucky one. By the way, the odds are greater that you would be hit twice by lightning in the same day than win the lottery.

Once I was in Lake Charles, Louisiana, and my host told me the best restaurant in town was at Harrah's Casino. So I graciously went along. He was right! The food was delicious, but there was something eerie and uncomfortable about being in the building itself. The halls were lined with pictures of advertisements depicting happy faces of people who had won big. The faces were so overly happy that it was surreal.

After dinner we were sitting at a table and eating ice cream outside the restaurant. I couldn't help but notice two elderly people at another table. The woman was counting quarters, and when she stopped, she threw her hands up in frustration and began to weep. The man dropped his head. As the two departed, it was very apparent to me that they had lost a large amount of money. My heart simply ached for these two as they slowly and sadly trudged away, having left behind perhaps their life's savings in hopes of moving to easy street.

I began to observe adults of all ages and races and from all walks of life as they entered the main hallway leading to the casino. All were upbeat and smiling. Some were even laughing and holding hands, but even a casual observer could readily tell a marked difference between the countenances of those leaving and those going in. The ones going in just knew this would be the day they would beat the house. The ones coming out were tasting the bitterness of disappointment at being suckers. Some looked as though they had been suddenly frightened at the realization of how quickly they had squandered their money—maybe even maxing out a credit card or *several*. Nobody coming out was laughing or holding hands; there were only the somber, stunned faces of losers. Some couples were arguing and angry, maybe blaming each other for their foolishness.

The gambling industry with its flashing neon lights, beautiful hotels, and entertainment promises easy money and instant wealth, but what many people get is personal bankruptcy.

Churches and government-aid offices report an alarming increase in the number of women asking for assistance, food, or medicine for their children. They are without the financial means to provide anything because their husbands have spent the weekly paycheck on lottery tickets.

Men and women who live week to week are the ones most suscep-tible to the *lure*. They believe the slick ads that show mansions with swimming pools and luxury cars, but in reality they lose more than their present finances can tolerate. The resulting demand on state social services is greater than can be met.

Enrollment in Gamblers Anonymous is growing each year, and new chapters are forming even in the smallest of towns. More and more families are being torn apart by an addicted gambler who becomes obsessed to a dangerous point and experiences an emotional meltdown. The innocent are often victims of gambling too, as home life becomes unbearable physically, emotionally, and mentally.

In low-income neighborhoods, the innocent often die violently when competing gambling interests war against one another. Gamblers soon turn to alcohol or drugs in order to escape the reality of their actions, which only serves to heighten the severity for the family.

Gambling seems to course through a person's veins, much like an addictive drug, driving men and women to do unspeakable things to feed their addiction. During the video poker crisis in South Carolina, I personally saw two young children in a filthy home. Both were neglected and hungry. The oldest was about three years old. He was sitting on the floor, sucking his thumb, hollow-eyed, and ribs showing. The six-month-old baby was lying in the crib in his own vomit, stinking and dirty. Law enforcement found the mother at a nearby convenience store playing video poker. She was arrested for child endangerment and neglect. She began to cry and scream as her children were taken into protective custody.

A funeral director related the story of a young man who took the dress off his seven-year-old little girl as her body lay in a small casket. He then sold the dress for a few dollars to play video poker. I received a letter from a woman who told me a heart-wrenching story about a young mother of two who sat by her husband's bedside as he lay dying from injuries he had received in an automobile accident. In the last hour of his life, he struggled to tell his wife of his gambling addiction: that he had secretly spent all their savings, emptied their checking account, maxed out the credit cards, and second-mortgaged the house—all to finance his gambling. He had allowed his life insurance policy to lapse from nonpayment. He told her that when he was gone, she would be broke and homeless.

Make no mistake; gambling in any form is one of the most destructive forces to the families in our nation. Constant losing causes people who are addicted to lose all perspective. They will resort to criminal activity, acts they would normally have been horrified to even hear the suggestion of committing. The gamblers' personal situations become desperate as they frantically attempt to recover their losses before the bills come due or the family discovers what they are involved in.

The corrupting influence of gambling changes a person's character. People become consumed by the insatiable desire to become a millionaire, and the decent personality traits they once possessed soon disappear and are replaced by deceit, lying, manipulation, fraud, and coldheartedness. Those drastic changes in character are a prelude to a downward plunge into personal catastrophe.

No, gambling is not harmless entertainment. Family counselors will tell you that broken homes, ruined credit, dysfunctional children, and shame are the by-products of a gambler who has gone over the edge.

Gambling tends to rob people of initiative and the necessary incentive in life, which is *to be successful we must work at a vocation. We must earn it.* There are no free rides. Anything that robs a family of its financial livelihood is not recreation. It's a seductive addiction that bankrupts both the individual and the family involved.

State lawmakers have bought into the concept of using gambling as a means to raise money in order to further fund education. But the word *education* is used to get gullible people to support gambling. Year after year in states where lotteries and gambling are legalized, we hear one excuse after another about how this year the proceeds from gambling just won't be enough. We didn't clear what we expected to. And why is that? Simple — because states open themselves up to companies that operate gambling and its related problems, including the expensive advertising and payouts to the ticket sellers, as well as the huge cuts the gambling companies take right off the top. It is believed that of every $100 collected in lottery sales, 90 percent will be spent dealing with the vices that accompany legalized gambling.

It is not about an alternate way to generate additional state income. State-sponsored gambling has proven itself to be an overall failure. When a state chooses to sanction gambling, it entices its legislators to get a piece of the action, to become involved in an illegal way. Look at the state of New Jersey for a prime example of where legalized gambling takes state government. New Jersey has probably the most corrupt state government in America, and people continue to support it because the majority of citizens have themselves been corrupted. The temptation exists for politicians to be too closely associated, thereby impairing their judgment.

It is a widely known fact in the gambling industry that a certain amount of profit is set aside as payoffs to dishonest politicians and lottery commission board members. It has been proven time and again that when all the accounting is complete, lotteries do not help state budgets in any significant way. Those who say it does are lying.

The business community hates legalized gambling. Why? Because they know gamblers will gamble money that should be spent purchasing needed products. Businesses, especially small businesses, recognize immediately the impact wholesale gambling has on their bottom line and how it will ultimately affect their very survival.

As attorney general, the late Robert Kennedy made a statement that was carried by all the national media. Here is what he said: "No one knows just how much money is spent on gambling in America. What we do know is this: some American people are spending more on gambling than they are spending on medical care or education; that in doing so, they are providing the money for corruption of public officials and the vicious activities of drug dealers, high-interest loans, illegal liquor, and prostitution." Now keep in mind, Robert Kennedy made this statement in 1962—forty-five years ago! One must pause to wonder how much greater the negative impact is today.

Gambling always attracts society's worst elements to host cities, and those cities inevitably lose their integrity and decent way of life. The overall quality of life changes considerably in states and towns where gambling and lotteries are legal. The Gulf Coast towns that used to be quaint villages with shops lining the streets have now been replaced by a neon jungle. Gone forever is the quaint, simple way of life that those residents once enjoyed. It is just ridiculous to believe that a state can remain the same when it embraces gambling. Streets are frequented by bums seeking a handout, and men who were once good citizens now are winos and lying on sidewalks.

Yes, government may collect a few dollars, and it may even point to some meaningless economic gain; but the counted cost to the spiritual, moral, and social climate of its citizens is way too high a price to pay for a measly few dollars of state income.

Lawmakers seem to have a memory lapse when the subject is legalized gambling. They owe the general public a moral responsibility as well as an economic one. State legislators, though, continue to voice the same pathetic argument. That is, we must have lotteries and gambling in order to make up budget deficits so that states can prosper. Any society that depends upon the addictive weaknesses of its people to exist does not deserve to survive.

Given the naïveté of America's populace, gambling will probably always be a fact of life. We need to educate future generations about its pitfalls and dangers and point to the dire effects it's having on our present generation. We must encourage them to avoid gambling as though it were a plague. Because when all is considered, it really is.

It is redefining the way to success, and that something-for-nothing philosophy will kill the work ethic in America.

Chapter 11

Liberal Power-Hungry Politicians
Cloaked as Public Servants

—〰—

I want to begin this chapter by telling you what I cannot accept about liberal politicians. It is not the way they look, where they live, the way they act, what they drive, or their political party. It's their *thinking*. They don't think like the majority of us in America. Why? They don't think with reason. Liberals form an opinion based on personal ideology and never on facts.

It's amazing that they can watch the daily news or read *USA Today* and continue to promote and fund their agenda. How can they not recognize the fact that they are so out of step with America and in lockstep with secular progressive idiots? Why is it so hard for liberals to consider even for a moment that they could be taking America down a road from which there is no return?

In other words, *This is the way I think, so don't confuse me with facts.* I watched Teresa Heinz Kerry's speech at the Democratic "reinvention" convention. Now, basically 95 percent of what she said was meaningless. The other 5 percent was partisan shots. Yet as the cameras spanned the faces of the delegates, they were glassy-eyed in admiration and fawned over her with smiles and applause.

Why did they believe her speech was so wonderful? That is the way followers of liberals think. There does not have to be any substance, truth, or reason. That is just the way liberals think. I find it so interesting that liberal politicians always seem to be for what the rest of us are against, and against what the rest of us see as correct.

Senator John Kerry invited us to check the record on his votes concerning national defense. Now remember, 73 percent of the people in America fully support an able and equipped defense program. I checked; here is how John Kerry voted. He voted to kill the B-1, the B-2, and the Patriot antimissile system that was used so effectively in Desert Storm. He voted against the F-18 and the F-117. He voted no on the Bradley fighting machine and the M-1 Abrams tank. Kerry voted against each bill appropriating funds for the development and deployment of *every* weapons system. He has been voting against those much-needed systems each year since 1988. He has a long record of being against what the majority of America is for. Kerry even voted no on supplying troops with battle armor. He voted against every proposed aircraft carrier and the Aegi's antiaircraft system. These are weapons that give us the capability to defend our freedom.

The rest of us in America have come to fully understand the threat terrorists pose to our safety. John Kerry voted against law enforcement and investigative arms of the government (FBI, CIA) having additional funds to fight the war on terror. He voted to cut the funding of the FBI by 60 percent, the NSA by 80 percent, and the CIA by 80 percent. It's no wonder they failed to provide protection and intelligence!

Kerry seemed more interested in becoming popular on the international scene than in protecting America. He voted to increase U.S. participation in the United Nations by a whopping *800 percent!* Thankfully, he lost his bid for the White House. The Swift boat men got it right when they said that he was "unfit to command."

There it is! Liberal politicians are against that which is so evident to the rest of us. Yet they are for what everyone else sees as a ridiculous position to take. Our frustration comes from how their thinking can be so far removed from reason and then we must live with the after-effects. I have been giving a lot of thought to the issues in America that most impact our lives. I began to examine the contrast between liberal thinking and the thinking of reasonable people, and I can assure you without a doubt, we are poles apart. Let's do a comparison on the issues so you can see the unorthodox thinking of liberal power-hungry politicians.

Senate liberals led by Hillary Clinton, Diane Feinstein, and ultra-liberal Harry Reid recently attempted to silence conservative radio talk shows by reinstating the "fairness doctrine." The public outcry was swift and loud. Congress, not wishing to further anger the electorate, voted 309 to 115 to stop funding that would be earmarked to reinstate the fairness doctrine.

Why would they try to do such a thing? Because conservative radio keeps liberals from getting by with telling the American people lies. In short, they expose these secular progressives for what they are. That certainly is not good for politicians with hidden agendas.

This ill-advised attempt by Clinton and her cronies would have guaranteed the federal government the power to censor free speech and thought through radio broadcasts. *Air America,* the Far Left's version of talk radio, went bankrupt. I wonder why. Could it be that an overwhelming majority of Americans are not Far Left and would not support their antimilitary, anti-president, and anti-American rhetoric? You bet it is. Will the liberal Left ever wake up? I doubt it!

We have established that the majority of Americans clearly understand that a strong military ensures our safety as a nation. The liberal thinks the military should be seen, but not heard; put on display, but not into action. The liberal politician is almost embarrassed that we even have a military, apologizing to the rest of the world because we are so mighty. Liberals think that if given the choice, it would be better to surrender and have world peace.

I am reminded of what Sir Winston Churchill said: "An appeaser is one who feeds a crocodile, hoping that it will eat him last." Liberals are more interested that the military be politically correct than fully funded. Anybody with an ounce of sense and knowledge of past history realizes how dangerous this type of thinking is, especially in a world that has become a powder keg where lunatics run around with torches ready to light the fuse.

When Al-Qaeda struck on September 11, they wrongly assumed that Americans would run into the streets begging for mercy. Where did they get that idea? From Al Gore, who wanted to have a dialogue with Osama, and from Madelyn Albright, the most inept secretary of state ever. During the Clinton years, these two represented America to international thugs who surmised, and rightly so, that we were weak, because we were being represented by a thumb-sucking, tree-hugging pacifist and a doting woman who called the killers in Bosnia "meanies." No wonder they took us for wimps and cowards! After all, the most powerful nation on Earth surely would not send those two to represent them.

Evil minds will always be at work in this world to expand their dictatorships, kingdoms, and regimes. We must ensure their conquests don't include America. Most Americans are unaware that the American Muslim Task Force of Civil Rights and Elections was provided a hospitality suite by liberal Democrats at the Democratic convention. Does that make you nervous? Well, try this! Al-Jazeera television, which is Osama bin Laden's mouthpiece, was also given a booth at the Fleet Center, where they took great delight in broadcasting Bush-bashing to the Arab Muslims back home. If that doesn't infuriate you, nothing will. This is the same Al-Jazeera television that was kicked out of Iraq by the new Iraqi government. The new leaders saw Al-Jazeera as a propaganda arm that threatened peace in Iraq.

Liberals think that respect should be handed out and not earned, that Americans should readily accept and adopt the liberal agenda and ask no questions—the "We will take care of you, don't worry about it" philosophy. How dare we question their integrity or motives! That would be downright villainous on our part.

Liberals think that bloated, wealthy bureaucrats such as Ted "Chappaquiddick" Kennedy, John "I married money" Kerry, and John "I sued for mine" Edwards are really in touch with the plight of the average working American who weekly labors eight to ten hours a day and has a third of his or her paycheck taken by the government.

Hillary Clinton is floating the concept of a society where those who have, share equally with those who don't, with the goal being for all of us to be on the same level financially. How will this gran-diose scheme be achieved? Why, through more taxation, of course.

I believe that elected officials should heed the advice of former President Calvin Coolidge in his inaugural address to the nation on March 4, 1925. Here is what he said: "The collection of any taxes which are not absolutely required, which do not beyond reasonable doubt contribute to the public welfare, is only a species of legalized larceny. . . . The wise and correct course to follow in taxation is not to destroy those who have already secured success, but to create conditions under which everyone will have a better chance to be successful."

The great statesman Thomas Jefferson addressed the issues of taxation and social welfare programs thusly: "To compel a man to furnish contributions of money for the propagation of opinion which he disbelieving and abhors is sinful and tyrannical. . . . A wise and frugal government . . . shall not take from the mouth of labor the bread it has earned. . . . Congress has not unlimited powers to provide for the general welfare but only those specially enumerated. . . . Would it not be better to simplify the system of taxation rather than spread it over such a variety of subjects and pass through so many new hands?" How we need statesmen like these men today!

Liberals think that just because other liberals say, "I feel your pain," they actually do. I am always astounded at how easily liberals believe fairy tales and the absurd but cannot process the truth, no matter what. Liberal power-hungry politicians think we should not have the right to bear arms. They think that "old mean guns" kill innocent people. But not for one moment do they stop to think that a gun must be in the hands of a person who intends to kill.

Liberals oppose the National Rifle Association because it lays full claim to our constitutional right to bear arms. Liberals think that law-abiding citizens who hold jobs, raise their families, help their neighbors, and attend church are dangerous people who cannot be trusted to possess firearms. They believe that if guns are banned, all the robbers, murderers, rapists, and gang members just won't have guns. Hello! Somebody please turn the lights on; the house is dark.

Immediately after every senseless shooting of innocent people, liberals crowd around microphones in groups to once again rail against guns. Shamelessly they use a human tragedy as fodder to stoke the fire for those who support the concept of disarming gun owners. There are people who possess guns only to protect their families and maybe even their country from the advance of international killers. Secular progressive liberals also see game hunters as a dangerous lot that needs to be gunless.

America's armed populace was possibly the main factor in averting a planned invasion of the United States by Nikita Khrushchev of Russia. Khrushchev met early one morning with his cabinet and shocked them by pronouncing that he wanted to attack the United States and invade her. His cabinet members were stunned.

Finally, one timid Russian said, "We cannot."

Khrushchev slammed his fist on the table and roared, "Why not?"

The man said, "Because we will not just be fighting the military. The American people are armed, and they will spill into the streets and fight till the death for their families, their way of life, and their freedom." [Russian Chronicles]

Nikita Khrushchev slumped back in his chair and never mentioned invading America again. Now you see how vital our constitutional right to bear arms really is. But liberal politicians don't think so. They don't think like we do.

Liberals think they are social engineers building a better America for everybody when they tax working people to death and spend millions on government giveaway programs for bums, but they do understand that these bums will register and vote for them if the handouts keep coming. That's why liberal Democrats are soft on the idea of toughening immigration laws. Some go so far as to advocate open borders.

Most immigrants vote Democrat. Why shouldn't they? These liberals will give them handouts from the government money pot in exchange for their votes. It does not matter how unfair it is to the taxpayers in America. Liberals will offer both legal and illegal aliens *free* health care, no-interest business loans, tax forgiveness, incentives to buy houses, and education that provides *everything free*.

Make no mistake about this; liberals believe that illegals should enjoy more of the American dream than Americans who work every day, pay taxes, and pray that through hard work their ship will come in or at the very least they will have enough to retire on. If these new-rank liberals have their way, the working American won't live to see either.

Liberal politicians think private businesses and corporations create a type of prosperity that offends the have-nots. They don't stop to think that without business corporations and company owners, there would be no jobs for anybody.

Liberal politicians purport a socialistic view. They think that government is better suited to control commerce and provide jobs. Well, you know what? That has been tried in other countries where poverty, corruption, and death are the norm. Private enterprise has made America economically strong, but the big government of liberal politicians has always hindered the free enterprise system in America.

The mantra for liberals is this: *we will tax the rich and make everybody equal*, but they never do. They raise taxes on everybody. Liberals just don't get the fact that the rich provide jobs and benefits for millions of people. It's not a crime to have money. Not everybody in America is going to be wealthy. Liberal politicians think they have a good idea of how to make voters like them: by bashing the wealthy while at the same time making millions themselves and finding every loophole they can to avoid paying a fair share of taxes. That is the height of hypocrisy, but so typical of liberals.

Liberal power-hungry politicians are incensed at the meteoric rise of talk radio and the rise of fair and balanced cable news. You see, for years the liberal agenda has gone unopposed in the media. They have been supported by the likes of Dan Rather and Katie Couric. Liberals could take comfort and always count on the news coverage to be biased and slanted to the left. Now they think it's a right-wing conspiracy to present the public with the other side of an issue. Liberals see Fox News as a troublemaker and anti-liberal, rather than a fresh medium that can be trusted to present the truth.

I thought Jay Leno's take on the *Tonight Show* was both funny and insightful. He asked this question: "If Hillary Clinton, Barak Obama, and John Edwards say they will not participate in a presidential debate because the debate is on Fox News and Fox News is biased, how are they going to stand up to terrorists when they're afraid of Fox News?"

Liberal power-hungry politicians will spend millions to rehabilitate a pedophile and then release him into an unsuspecting neighborhood, when in reality, the criminal has not changed one bit. They will fight for the rights of rapists and armed robbers to have television sets, stereos, and porn magazines in prison cells, but

they will not appropriate one dime for police vests or crime preven-
tion. Liberals will squall and wail for a cold-blooded killer who is
executed, lighting candles and singing; but they oppose the right of
a victim's family to testify at the sentencing phase of a trial. Why?
They think that will influence the jury. Well, yeah!

To the liberals, serial killers are simply a product of their environment, and it's society's fault that they are the way they are. Liberals
seek to pass laws that protect criminals' rights, while proclaiming
that law enforcement officers are a Gestapo that should be watched
carefully. Liberal politicians believe police work should have a pacifist approach. In other words, be nice to the crack addict with the
knife and he will reciprocate and be nice also. What junk!

During Oliver North's Contra hearings, liberal politicians,
especially Al Gore, saw North as a serious threat to America. They
laughed when Colonel North testified that Osama bin Laden was the
most dangerous man in the world.

On almost every single important issue, liberals are on the wrong
side. They think that a partially educated, underqualified public
school teacher, who is divorced, has a pregnant teen daughter and

a teen son smoking pot, and who cannot adequately teach a third-grader how to read, is still highly qualified to teach sex education.

Liberal power-hungry politicians, especially Democrats who fall into that category, knock themselves out in order to cater to every radical black organization in America. They seem to be mesmerized by the opportunity to do a photo op with Jesse Jackson and Al Sharpton. I intentionally left out the "reverend" part as it routinely applies to these two.

Liberal politicians think the Pope, Franklin Graham, and Pat Robertson should stay out of politics, but it's okay for half of the black churches in America to invite all the liberal Democrats to church and dinner. They think organizations that hate blacks are racist (and they are). The white-hating Black Panthers, are **not racist**? They are just *expressing frustration* over slavery? Well, I for one have had about all I can take in one lifetime of this rotten double standard.

Liberal politicians preach that all conservatives are dead set against blacks advancing in life, while simultaneously preaching that blacks cannot make it without the help of "Daddy Liberal."

As Election Day approached, a liberal politician was overheard saying, "I don't want to buy the black vote; I just want to rent it for a day." *[The State News]* How about that for sincerity!

Liberals were indignant about Mel Gibson's movie *The Passion of the Christ,* railing about how offensive it was and how it was just a Christian's version about Jesus and certainly not factual. They believed it portrayed Jews in a negative light, but these same liberals applauded Michael Moore's dishonest film about President Bush as the pure truth and a courageous production. Go figure! That is the way liberals think. If they all lived in the same state, you might say it was the drinking water that has affected their thinking. But they don't, so obviously it's just the way they choose to think.

Former president Jimmy Carter is what I consider the most deluded and dangerous of liberals. When it comes to reality, Carter has always been an ignorant man. The fact that he is a former president adds to the disgrace that he has brought upon himself, his country, and Israel.

Carter's speech in Europe was salted with invectives against the United States, convincing many that his words were treasonous. Then, in Reno, Nevada, he arrogantly proclaimed that President

George Bush has brought international shame to America. This came from a man who will go down in history as the most inept, confused, and pathetic president of our time.

His inaction during the Iran hostage crisis brought embarrassment to our once powerful nation and humiliation to the hostages as they bravely endured 444 days of captivity. Carter defended his inaction by saying that he was holding back in favor of diplomacy, but for him that was another word for cowardice.

His policies gutted the military and ruined the economy with nearly 20 percent inflation and the highest unemployment rate since the Great Depression. Mortgage interest rates soared to nearly 18 percent, making the dream of owning a home an illusion for many already struggling families. Carter's malaise fell over our nation like a blanket of death, and he was clueless as to what should be done.

His latest book, *Palestine: Peace Not Apartheid,* was so inaccurately offensive that it caused many longtime associates to finally abandon him. This book was the last straw. Fourteen members of his advisory board resigned from the Carter Center in a unified act of protest over the book's lies, inaccuracies, and obvious bias against tiny Israel's right to exist.

Others distanced themselves from him, no longer having the stomach for his Far Left ranting and not willing to be associated with his free fall from reason. In his criticism of Israel, Carter suffered historical memory loss by daring to downplay the awful reality of the Holocaust and the horrible sufferings of its victims. In so doing, he fueled the fires of terrorist hatred even more and gave encouragement to Israel's enemies.

Carter doesn't seem to care, though, as he continues to operate in his own world of delusion. His hypocrisy seems to know no bounds, as he even tried to pressure the Southern Baptist Convention into changing their long-held doctrines and beliefs to suit his liberal theological persuasion. He has ridiculed and derided some of the most respected religious leaders in America, somehow thinking that he could exert his own secular progressive religious sway over everybody else.

Jimmy Carter is a man who once rose to the pinnacle of political life in America but has now plummeted to the depths of a soured existence.

Liberals think new laws need to be enacted that elevate crimes against certain segments of society to a higher level of seriousness and punishment than crimes committed against you and me. This is cloaked as the hate crimes bill.

Now wait a minute. Let's understand this. If somebody beats the daylights out of the average Joe just for meanness, or Bubba beats up another Bubba at the country dance, then that is just your garden-variety crime. If a man uses a gun and kills his estranged wife and his children, that's just a simple murder of passion; but if somebody attacks a homosexual just because he wants to or slaps a gay for propositioning him or her, then that is a hate crime. How in the world?

A crime is a crime. Anybody who kills another person is full of hate. Any person who arbitrarily beats up people is full of hate toward other humans. This is a dangerous law being pushed by liberals and should never be passed. The hate crimes law is a clear violation of Section 10 of the Fourteenth Amendment to the United States Constitution.

Liberal politicians can easily understand when a homosexual is murdered by a straight person that it should be an outrage. But they think crimes against the rest of our society committed by law-breaking homosexuals should go virtually unnoticed.

A chilly and what we can only pray won't be a precedent-setting incident took place at Pace University in New York City. A twenty-three-year-old male student, tired of Muslim students harassing him, took a Koran out of the common room and then tried to flush it down the toilet. The university reprimanded the student for a simple act of vandalism. And that was the end of it, as it should have been.

But after extreme pressure from CAIR (the Council on American and Islamic Relations), a radical Muslim organization that is funded by power-hungry Saudi princes who want to take over the world for Islam, the university allowed itself to be bullied and called the police to investigate it as a hate crime.

It was a book, for God's sake, not a person. Cite the student and make him pick up trash on campus for a week, but charge him with a federal crime? Talk about overkill; talk about a total lack of clear thought. This is it.

I cannot begin to tell you how serious and dangerous it is to every American when radical Muslims can dictate punishment to those who oppose their religion, making unreasonable demands upon institutions or government to severely punish as a hate crime any form of dissent from Islam.

228

Liberal power-hungry politicians think American terrorists, such as Greenpeace, are doing a noble work. They think weirdos who climb trees in order to prevent forests from being thinned are heroes. However, thinning is done to prevent out-of-control forest fires from destroying everything and threatening neighborhoods.

Liberals propose and pass laws to prevent deer from being hunted on public lands. Deer then overpopulate, become diseased, and starve. Some die crossing highways, searching for food, and cause people to be killed in those collisions.

If a conservative politician is caught in wrongdoing, liberals rush to castigate him or her. You can hear them loudly calling for a resignation and piously pointing the finger, strutting like peacocks as if they had just saved the planet. On the other hand, when a conservative politician points out the wrongdoings committed by a liberal, they scream, "It is all just political."

Sandy Berger's raiding of the National Archives will certainly be recorded in history as one of the greatest examples of how liberals think. Berger stuffed documents in his pants and socks. Documents, I believe, that incriminated the Clinton administration in nonaction on terrorism. When caught in the underhanded deed, Berger said, "I made a mistake."

Now, the dictionary defines the word *mistake* as "a blunder," "an error." Berger *intentionally* went into the archives and took the documents. That's *not* an error. Give me a break!

The liberals ignored the wrongdoing and said, "It's political." They diverted attention from Berger's dishonest act and began to denigrate the people who turned him in, claiming they were political opportunists exploiting the moment. If that were you and I who went into the archives and took documents, we would be in jail. Do you see the pattern? Liberals cover their dirty messes by turning attention to those who blow the whistle, but they never acknowledge wrongdoing.

As you can see from comparing the way the majority of America thinks with liberal thinking, there is a stark contrast. We are so far apart. Liberals are the antithesis of reasoned thought. Liberal power-hungry politicians seek power as if it were the air they breathe. They will do anything to achieve power and stay in power.

The problem is, when they are in power and holding political offices across America, they always seem to abuse it, flaunting the public's trust. You see, they just don't get it. A position of power and influence that is bestowed upon a politician by the voters is to be used responsibly and for the good of the people, not to further personal agendas and interests.

Power-hungry politicians use their entire time in office to cut deals and ensure their re-election rather than provide legislation that solves the myriad of problems that confront the American people. To keep themselves in power, they hire people like James Carville, who is the epitome of a hateful liberal. Carville thinks he's intelligent when he guffaws and belittles good people. Carville and those like him should be banned from politics for attempting to smear others just because they offer an opposing view or belong to an opposing party. When I saw Carville ranting during the past election, it brought to mind a rabid Chihuahua under a strobe light. That is how out of control he appeared to be.

I firmly believe that liberal politicians have somehow convinced themselves that the only way to save America is for them to be in absolute power. Now there is a thought that will rob you of a sound sleep! We all know that absolute power corrupts absolutely. From the local level all the way to Washington, time and again we have observed liberals abusing power at the expense of citizens. They just cannot seem to grasp the concept that being a politician means holding an office of trust and service, not to be confused with being anointed king.

In the event that Hillary Clinton should become president (God forbid), Bill Clinton has expressed the desire to be secretary of the United Nations. From that position, he hopes to be president of the world. That thought will surely curdle your morning coffee, won't it?

The popularity game liberal politicians are playing on the international scene is the most dangerous of all. Those efforts to cozy up to suspect foreign governments will prove to be devastating to our national security.

President Bush, believing (and rightly so) that foreign policy should be handled by him or the secretary of state, objected to House Speaker Nancy Pelosi's planned meeting with Syrian President Assad, a known international political criminal. But Pelosi went anyway, complete with her symbolic head scarf. I guess she wanted to give the impression that she is sensitive to their cause. I sure get that impression.

What Pelosi really did was tamper with sensitive diplomatic negotiations that she knew nothing about. But a power-hungry liberal has never been stopped by such a small thing as a lack of knowledge, especially when there is an opportunity to pander to the Far Left. Her trip was ill-conceived and a possible violation of federal law.

Mrs. Pelosi even went so far as to deliver a message to Assad from Prime Minister Olmert of Israel. The message declared that Israel desired peace talks, but according to the White House, Olmert denied ever giving Pelosi a message to deliver. He further stated that he did not recognize Pelosi as on official representative of United States foreign policy.

Pelosi, though, is loyal to her constituents. This type of behavior is just what San Francisco applauds while the rest of us see her as an idiot playing a dangerous game of cat and mouse with two volatile nations, not to mention the confusion that she created by those who actually thought that she spoke for the United States government.

Liberals want to be friends with France, knowing full well that France has been trying to undermine U.S. foreign policy for thirty-five years. They want to sidle up to an unstable Germany, who has proven over and over that they cannot be trusted. Russia is chin deep in international corruption, from their backdoor deals with the now deceased Saddam Hussein to selling weapons to Iran and Syria.

But most disturbing are liberals who travel this country undermining the war effort in the Middle East. They are aiding and abetting an enemy that will be relentless in attempting to blow up our buildings and stall our economy. Israel, a tiny nation surrounded by people who want to kill every Jew, is seen by liberals as causing unrest in the Middle East. How? By just wanting to live like the rest of us.

How does any sane, reasonable person arrive at that conclusion? Just by being a liberal. That's all it takes. That will do it. These political dunces don't seem to care about how their careless speeches are used against our fighting men and women. It hurts morale and further adds fuel to the fires burning in the minds of lunatics. *Power is the goal; achieve it any way you can—* that is the clarion call of a liberal.

John Murtha and Senate Majority Leader Harry Reid are prime examples of politicians who push their personal ideologies without any regard for how it affects the country and our troops in Iraq.

The September 11 Commission cleared President Bush of any international wrongdoing, but facts mean nothing to liberals. They continue saying, "Bush lied and he misled us." Truth is irrelevant when they want to parrot a lie that may ultimately benefit liberalism politically.

Liberal politicians think that turning over control of the United States to the United Nations is a must-do. Please get this! When that happens, we lose our sovereignty as a nation, and given the expressed hatred toward America by rogue nations, that will be the beginning of the end for us. We will no longer have the right to make military decisions that are in our best interests.

Why, in God's name, would they do that? You say, Power! They desire power on the international scene, and that translates into power of personal millions. Liberals want to be loved by the world, and they will quickly jeopardize America to be loved by other countries. They wrongly believe that the opinions other nations hold of us are far more important than what is in the best interest of America's people. It is downright scary that elected politicians in the United States could even for a moment entertain an idea such as that.

Power is the elixir that dulls the mind and short-circuits the thought process of an ambitious liberal who seeks his or her own path rather than the well-traveled road of freedom. Cloaked as public servants, these misguided miscreants will kill our democracy if they are not removed from office.

Chapter 12

The ACLU

Maliciousness Cloaked in Civil Liberties

—៕—

The American Civil Liberties Union, an organization that cloaks itself in liberty but covertly reorders our society to open license (which is in reality licentiousness), has never been about civil liberties, but an uncivil mind-set. The word *American* in the title is a misnomer. Americanism is being partial to the things identified with the United States. There is nothing even remotely American about the ACLU. These bottom-feeders oppose any object, symbol, or idea that represents the real and historic America.

The ACLU is without a doubt the most dangerous organization operating in our society to date. When socialist Roger Baldwin founded the ACLU in 1919, he instructed those involved in the new ACLU movement to always pass themselves off as patriots and told his followers to preach about rights and liberty and fool the populace into thinking they were for America while covertly planning to dismantle the Constitution of the United States and eradicate Christianity from American life. Baldwin would be proud that this modern-day ACLU has done far worse and has exceeded his highest hopes.

Their idea of America is a nation gutted of godliness, decency, common sense, morals, standards, values, discipline, respect, honor, and justice. They desire an America that is a flowing sewer of every vile idea that the human mind can conjure up and an America where anything abhorrent is accepted, yet devoid of anything that serves as a marker or a guide to deter evil and its awful influences.

The ACLU is destroying acceptable behavior lawsuit by lawsuit. They do not care what kind of detrimental effect it will have on our society. The ACLU is without a conscience when it comes to even considering for a moment the far-reaching impact of their relentless war against America. They are numb to any true feeling for our nation.

Attorneys who represent the ACLU—at least the ones I have spoken to—seem to have an empty hole where there should be a heart and an empty head where there should be common sense. Their lust for money has overtaken reason.

The dictionary defines the word *civil* as "not military"; yet the ACLU has thrown down the gauntlet and openly declared war on Christianity in America. The second definition of *civil* is "not religious"; yet the ACLU is in principle a bigoted cult that directs its hatred toward all things Christian. The third definition is "polite." The ACLU is anything but polite. They are bullies and perpetual dictators, rewriting the Constitution to fit their own philosophy for the America they envision, attacking innocent organizations and individuals who are simply exercising their own rights.

The ACLU is modern-day gangsters who will do or say anything to achieve their purposes and to make millions of dollars along the way. Civil? I don't think so! They show a blatant disregard for what they put people through, or the costs exacted on taxpayers and the private legal fees incurred by the innocent to defend themselves.

The word *liberties* as used by the ACLU means "impertinence," which means "insolent"; and insolent means "disrespectful." The ACLU is without a doubt disrespectful of the rights of every person with whom they do not agree—disrespectful of the tenets

America was founded on, disrespectful of the Constitution as an old, outdated, yellowed paper, and disrespectful of the faith of millions of Christians.

The word *union* means "for mutual aid," but the only people profiting from civil liberties lawsuits are the ACLU, with a smirk on the face of those in whose names the lawsuits are filed: the anti-God, the anti-Christian, the child pornographer, the radical homosexual, the liberal professor, the purveyors of filth, the deluded atheist, the Muslim terrorist, and the ignorant anti-American.

"Why? Why?" people ask incredulously. What drives the ACLU to attack Christianity and every symbol that even remotely represents it? The answer is twofold. First, it is millions of dollars in legal fees. How do they collect? By a 1976 federal law that most Americans are unaware of. It is called the Civil Rights Attorney Fees Awards Act. The law was written in its original intent for states or the federal government to pay the fees of attorneys who filed legitimate civil rights cases, cases involving discrimination based on race, sex, or national origin. The law was designed to help plaintiffs in civil rights cases and to provide attorneys an avenue to collect fees.

The ACLU has seized upon this law and perverted the spirit of it in order to collect huge attorney fees for lawsuits filed against such dangerous threats to liberty as the words *In God We Trust,* the Pledge of Allegiance, crosses, a Christmas tree, and the Boy Scouts. The ACLU is flagrantly using this law for First Amendment cases, claiming piously that it is a person's civil right not to have to look at a cross or be offended by a place wherein is written the Ten Commandments.

The ACLU has discovered a cash cow created by perverting the law's original intent. That is the motivation to file lawsuits in every state, county, and city in America, filing lawsuits against public schools or any public venue that dares display any symbol that can be related to Christianity. With the abundance of states, cities, towns, schools, and parks in America, you can readily see the limitless potential to earn millions of dollars.

The ACLU is filing lawsuits all over America. In the state of Utah, the ACLU orchestrated a scavenger hunt for any object that would fall into their civil rights violation category. Anyone who reported a violation received a prize. In the business world, that is called drumming up business. If stooping to that level is not low-down and despicable, then I don't know what would qualify. Once an object is found, a suit is filed. Tyrannical judges order the object removed as they work hand in hand with the ACLU.

I mentioned the lawsuit against the Boy Scouts. In San Diego the Scouts, as was their right (and correctly so), forbade homosexuals from working as leaders in the Boy Scouts, thus making the decision to protect young boys from falling victim to gay pedophiles (who the ACLU supports, by the way). After that decision by the Boy Scouts, the ACLU redefined them as a religion. We knew that was coming in order for the lawsuit to qualify. Now you are about to become outraged if you are not already. The ACLU reaped a huge profit in collecting $790,000 in legal fees, plus $160,000 in court costs. But even worse, they succeeded in denying the Scouts the right as Americans to use Balboa Park for summer camps. Now remember, the Boy Scouts had used this park since 1915. That's eighty-nine years!

Why was it suddenly a violation of civil rights? The ACLU said so. The Boy Scouts did not deserve to use the park because they denied homosexuals leader status and because of the oath they dared utter: "to do my duty to God and my country."

How much longer are we going to stand quietly by and allow this to continue? We fought wars against people who were these kinds of enemies that threatened our freedom. Men and women gave their lives for the freedom to worship the God America was founded on. It is incumbent upon us to do everything in our power to educate the American people about an organization that is a real and present danger to liberty. We have never encountered within our walls a more sinister group. Because they are citizens of the United States, it heightens the threat to gargantuan proportions.

Alan Sears, a former federal prosecutor in the Reagan administration, said this: "One of the great myths of the twentieth- and twenty-first centuries is the belief that the ACLU was at one time an organization that had a noble beginning, but somehow strayed off course. That myth is untrue. The ACLU set a course to destroy America, her freedom, and her values, right from the start."

The ACLU sees money in every instance, no matter how insignificant. The ACLU railroaded the supervisors of Los Angeles County to yield and remove a small, negligible cross from the Los Angeles county seal. Even after the county was offered free legal defense, these spineless wonders folded their tents and gave in to what will be a cost of millions of dollars to remove the cross.

What about the rights of all the other people in Los Angeles County? I guess their rights did not matter. I say again, how much longer are we going to allow these arrogant bullies to destroy our heritage? Let me describe the Los Angeles county seal that was so offensive. All the symbols centered on the Greek goddess Pomona, depicted standing by the Pacific Ocean. But paganism is encouraged by the ACLU. The six-sided sections on the seal represent the Spanish galleon, San Salvador, a cow, the Hollywood Bowl, two stars for television and movies, a tuna fish, oil derricks, and several instruments used by engineers. The cross in question is very small, hardly noticeable, and harmless. What the ACLU noticed was a violation of the First Amendment according to their distorted and biased interpretation. It was yet another opportunity to collect while cloaking the whole sordid affair in a garment of liberty.

It's a fact! The ACLU has come up with a way to use government as a weapon against the people of this country. They want to reshape our society to fit their permissive bent and make millions in the process. What the ACLU is doing to freedom in America is akin to watching a train wreck in slow motion. It's agonizing.

The ACLU has a penchant for defending every threat to our democracy, safety, and spiritual life. If it's a man who supports terrorism, defend him. If it's a person who is a traitor to the United States, defend him.

If it's a child molester, defend him. What else can you expect when one of their own, fifty-one-year-old Russ Tierney, the former president of the Virginia ACLU, was charged with child pornography after law enforcement raided his home and found images of prepubescent girls being violently raped and tied up, screaming and crying?

If it's the perverted North American Man-Boy Love Association fighting for the right to have sex with children, the ACLU rushes to take action on these sickos' behalf. It is very disturbing that in every single case where children's rights are at stake, the ACLU advocates for child predators, those who absolutely destroy the lives of children.

NAMBLA is made up of men who, by society's standards, are morally filthy and sexually twisted. If they were anything but human, they would be fish guts. I realize that is a vivid analogy; but given the predilection of these people, it's an appropriate one.

NAMBLA puts out information to its members and others that describe in detail how to entice and trick innocent little boys into submitting themselves to awful sex acts that literally maim their bodies. Not only that, but the ACLU knows this sort of activity is illegal, so they coach these sexual leeches on what steps to take if their illegal deviant acts are discovered.

This illustration alone tells us just how sinister the ACLU really is. But there are other examples. Since passing as legislation, Megan's Law mandates registry of convicted sex offenders. This law was long overdue, but it has been continually challenged by the ACLU. The law was named after Megan Kanka, a New Jersey girl who was raped and murdered by a known child molester who lived right across the street from Megan's family, though they were unaware of his presence. This law is a serious and much-needed safeguard that will protect children in neighborhoods.

Because of national exposure by Bill O'Reilly on *The O'Reilly Factor* television program, Megan's Law was passed in all fifty states. Legislators, law enforcement, and parents hailed it as a giant step toward identifying those who wish to blend into society in order to molest again.

But as always, the ACLU saw the law as bad for *perverts* and pedophiles—innocent children be damned! Let's just not restrict the *rights* of those in society who are lurking around waiting for the opportunity to create a nightmare for a child and his or her family.

The ACLU argues to protect child pornography under "free speech," though the majority of child molestation cases, child pornography has been found to be the catalyst that inflames child stalkers. I ask you, Do America's children have a bigger enemy than the ACLU?

In Michigan the ACLU is fighting a computer program that will prevent possible terrorism. The program, Matrix, provides law enforcement with instant access to information on possible terrorist acts. The ACLU believes the program will be abused by authorities. If this program would have been in place, it would have prevented Ramzi Yousef from masterminding the World Trade Center bombing.

Do you see the pattern? The majority of Americans see all the things I've mentioned as destructive and undermining to our way of life, but the ACLU throws their arms around them.

Along the border, Arizona operatives for the ACLU are working against the Minutemen, a volunteer group that protects Arizona's border with Mexico from illegal aliens. When these operatives spot illegal immigrants attempting to cross the border at night near an area where the Minutemen are posted, they blare loud horns and flash car lights so the illegal immigrants will seek a safer crossing area.

Since entering the United States illegally is a federal crime, then it would also be illegal to help people violate the law; but the ACLU disregards that in favor of the pursuit of radical activism. Obviously, these fools don't stop to consider that one or more of those trying to sneak into America may very well be terrorists who are part of a plan to blow Americans up. But I submit, they don't care!

Every effort is being made by this organization to hinder officials from enforcing immigration laws, and they are doing that by hiding along the borders and filing ridiculous lawsuits in court.

The ACLU has been relentless in demonizing the Patriot Act, even though it has been proven to be instrumental in stopping terrorists' attacks aimed at the United States. Now in order to protect our well-being, there may be some inconveniences, but I submit that unless you are a terrorist seeking to kill Americans, then you don't have anything to be worried about. If your phone is not being used to make international calls to Osama bin Laden, then you're okay and won't be bothered.

If you are doing that and you are a suspect, then hopefully authorities will be able to use the clearly defined powers of the Patriot Act to catch your sorry behind and behead you—I mean arrest you—try you and put you in prison, and feed your loathsome face for the rest of your sorry life or until the Muslims take over America and free you, God forbid!

But in the meantime, you can surely count on your chums at the ACLU to try to make it difficult for law enforcement to catch you until you are successful at killing thousands of innocent Americans and blow yourself to hell.

ACLU, friend to terrorists everywhere, count on it!

The ACLU recently filed suit against the NSA (National Security Agency). Why? In order to *stop* counterterrorism measures such as no-fly lists that prevent terrorists from attempting to board flights.

This proves once again to all Americans that they are anti-America and anti-security for our nation, while cloaking themselves as champions of liberty.

I believe you will agree with me that the members of this organization are traitors of the worst sort. They are enjoying the fruits of American life and freedom while at the same time attempting to destroy it. The ACLU has millions of dollars with which they continue their treasonous ways, and they are aided by left-wingers such as George Soros. They were forced to decline $1.5 million from the Ford and Rockefeller foundations because they refused to give assurances that none of the money would go to underwriting terrorism.

The ACLU intends to investigate every school district in America to see if they can find anything that would come under the heading of an offense they could sue for. Most public schools in this country struggle on a year-to-year basis to survive financially. That does not matter to these money-grubbers. Their callousness is exceeded only by their greed. The ACLU has done more to remove discipline and respect from public schools than anything else. Unwarranted lawsuits and threats of lawsuits have created a climate of fear for public educators, and it's all done in the name of rights.

The second factor driving the ACLU is the destruction of Christianity. The ACLU is bigoted, intolerant, and filled with hatred for all things Christian, modern-day vigilantes who have no regard for God, Jesus, or those who worship Him. You would have to be a complete fool not to recognize what is going on with the ACLU and Christianity. Is it any other religion you ask? No! They say nothing about symbols of Islam, Hinduism, Buddhism, Judaism, or Satan worship. These are okay. It is Christianity they want to totally annihilate.

By their actions the ACLU is telling us: *You don't have a place in America anymore. You, your Jesus, and your God, we will relegate to the garbage dump of history. We will throw you into the hole of forgetfulness where you will be remembered no more. We will attack your prayers. We will rail against your valedictorians' free-speech rights to use God in speeches. We will scream about your attempts to put up a Christmas tree in the town square. We will gnash on you with our teeth for daring to put up a dangerous and vile manger scene. We will be incensed that you would pledge allegiance to the*

God by whom America has been blessed. We will attack you like ravenous animals for displaying those horrid Ten Commandments. We will vilify you for any attempt you make to incorporate any aspect, word, or phrase about God or Jesus into any public forum. We will deny you access to any public place if you embrace a religious doctrine that we have predetermined to be offensive. We will attack you and attack your churches and your stupid, backward religion. We will tolerate sodomy, child sex, drug use, inflammatory rap music, nakedness, hatefulness, terrorism and anybody else's right to do whatever they want, but we will not tolerate Christianity. We will erase your influence from society and we will pervert the Constitution so it offers you no protection, and along the way, we will make millions doing it! That's the real ACLU!

This alien beast has now spawned offspring who spew the same hatred for anything that represents Christianity. Barry Lynn heads up Americans United for the Separation of Church and State. Lynn is a former ACLU operative and a despicable weasel who believes it's cute to tout himself as a reverend. He attempts to further discredit Christianity by saying, *Look, I'm a reverend, but I'm anti-Christian.*

Mr. Lynn is a reverend all right, and a pied piper who loathes Christianity and will lead the unknowing to destroy America.

Barry Lynn had the pompous audacity to file a complaint with the IRS accusing Jerry Falwell of wrongly using his tax-exempt status to support President Bush. Lynn is a bona-fide hypocrite, and he knows it. Strangely absent are any complaints about Jesse Jackson's or Al Sharpton's supporting of Democrats, speaking at the Democratic national convention, and raising money for Democrats in black churches. In his narrow, little, foggy mind, Lynn denounces one and puts his stamp of approval on the other. Only a man blinded by hatred and on a mission to destroy could draw that conclusion.

Norman Lear and his People for the American Way are Christian-haters. Lear's America is a way that says Christians are not welcome. Christianity is the wrong way. Who do these cloakers think they are fooling? The lot of them are as guilty as can be of hating a religion that has done nothing against them. Through its doctrines and faith, Christianity has fashioned the greatest nation on Earth. It's a nation where they have the freedom to openly practice their intolerance and bigotry without being imprisoned or killed.

The time has come; the ACLU and its spawn must be stopped. Right-thinking people in this country must admit what is happening and accept the glaring fact of how wicked these people are to expend the energy they do to destroy one particular religion. Christianity has been the moral conscience of America since the founding of our nation. We cannot remove that and expect our society will be better, because it won't. These twisted minds think it will, but it won't.

I have often thought if we sit back and are too apathetic to care, what will the ACLU and such organizations go after when all the symbols of Christianity and God are gone? Allow me to present the scenario for you. They will characterize Christian churches as preaching hate. They will sue to take tax-exempt status away. They will lobby for laws to have pastors imprisoned for hate speech and subverting society. They will sue to close Christian bookstores that sell Bibles. They will stop Christian concerts in public places. They will engage the FCC in a war to ban Christian broadcasts on television and radio. The ACLU will define flying a Christian flag in your yard as a crime that should be punished. They will sue to have all Christian material removed from public libraries. Where will they go from there? Well, just let your imagination run wild.

Each session of Congress begins with prayer by a minister who is paid by the taxpayers. When you ascend the steps of the building where the Supreme Court is located, at the top of that building is a row of the world's lawgivers. Every one of them is facing toward Moses, and his figure is holding the Ten Commandments. If you go inside the Supreme Court building, look at the wall above where the justices sit. There is a display of the Ten Commandments. You would be amazed, as I was, at how many Bible verses are imprinted into the stone walls of federal buildings and monuments all over the city of Washington, D.C. Did our founding fathers intend to build America on Christian values and the Bible? Absolutely! Without a doubt! The proof is everywhere in the capital city.

Does that matter to the ACLU? No! How long will it be before these "new society" dictators decide to sue the federal government to have all the inscriptions removed? It is just a matter of time. America was founded as "one nation under God." That was the intent of its founders. There is not one line in the United States Constitution that even remotely refers to what the ACLU claims. They simply made it say "separation of church and state." How? They looked for what they considered a loophole.

255

In a letter to the Danbury Baptist Association of Danbury, Connecticut, dated January 1, 1802, Thomas Jefferson allayed the fears of the Baptists by stating the First Amendment to the Constitution guaranteed complete protection from government interfering in religion. Here is what Jefferson said: "Believing with you that religion is a matter which lies solely between man and his God, that he owes account to none other for faith or his worship, that the legislative powers of government reach actions only, and not opinions, I contemplate with solemn reverence that act of the whole American people which declared that their legislature should make no laws respecting an establishment of religion, or prohibiting the free exercise thereof, thus building a wall of separation between church and state."

English and history scholars who have made exhaustive studies of this letter have agreed that the interpretation is crystal clear. Jefferson was assuring the people that government would not dictate and establish a totalitarian religion, that government could not legislate a religious doctrine that would be forced upon every American. You must have a hidden agenda, as the ACLU does, to make this letter and the First Amendment say anything other than that.

The ACLU has wrested from this letter and the Constitution a meaning that is unique only to the ACLU and those few radicals who embrace their view. The writings on landmarks, documents, and money offer proof positive that the founders meant for America to be a Christian nation and for government to have no right to develop a national religion and ruthlessly force it on Christians. Patrick Henry said, "It cannot be emphasized too strongly or too often that this great nation was founded not by religionists, but by Christians. Not on multiple religions, but on the Gospel of Jesus Christ."

The ACLU has taken extreme liberties with history. Our nation has lived by godly precepts for 220 years, but the all-knowing ACLU has decided that all the framers of our nation's laws were idiots and that we are a bunch of fools violating the Constitution. Daniel Webster said, "If there is anything in my thoughts or style to commend, the credit is due to my parents for instilling in me an early love of the Scriptures. If we abide by the principles taught in the Bible, our country will go on prospering; but if we and our posterity neglect its instructions and authority, no man can tell how sudden a catastrophe may overwhelm us and bury all our glory in profound obscurity."

Never before in history has an organization in America been as blatant about distorting every principle our country was founded on. The ACLU is that organization. I was told by my grandmother, "If it's not the truth, it's a lie." The ACLU is lying when they say the First Amendment of the Constitution of the United States was written to forbid Christianity from enjoying its rightful place in the establishing of America and its perpetuation. They are lying when they say the wall is there to keep Christians out of America. No! The wall Jefferson spoke so eloquently about was to keep dictators like the ACLU from prohibiting the influences of Christianity and its impact for good on America.

The ACLU is lying when they say that "Thou shalt not kill" and "Thou shalt not steal" are offensive and should not be displayed. Why are they so afraid of the commandments? Any right-thinking person can see these as a teaching tool to a younger generation.

The ACLU lies when they purport to be protecting America while their actions reveal otherwise. They are lying when they cloak themselves in liberty yet exhibit a malicious hatred toward every single principle that you or I find vital to the well-being of an individual, a marriage, a home, a church, and our nation.

The ACLU wields a dagger that plunges deep into the heart of America. Unless they are stopped, the ACLU will play the lead role in dismantling our system of justice, discipline, worship, decency, education, and the right to defend ourselves as a free nation.

In *News with Views,* August 16, 2003, there was an article by Hans Zeiger, a columnist for the *Seattle Times.* He wrote this:

> To the drugged up senses of the ACLU, citizenship is a rotting archaic concept. National unity and patriotism are outmoded values. Duty, honor, and country are the relics of dead generals that have yet to be sued out of school history books in some not-too-distant lawsuit campaign.
>
> Liberty is to be replaced with license and justice with favoritism to the devoid of truth. And then the red, white, and blue will cease to wave because of neglect. It will be the ACLU that presides over the final lowering of shredded Old Glory if ever that day comes.

The ACLU is malice cloaked in liberty. Their thinking is an intellectually borne pathogen that will poison and kill this body we call America.

Chapter 13

Planned Parenthood, Murder of the Unborn, and Radical Sex Education

Cloaked as Caring and Compassion

lanned Parenthood sounds innocent enough, right? Surely they are helping people to plan upcoming parenthood—maybe providing parents with valuable resources to raise happy families or teaching young couples how to plan for the day they will decide to have a baby. That's what you would expect from an organization that calls itself Planned Parenthood, but you would be wrong. The title is part of the cloak.

I have written about a number of organizations in this book; Planned Parenthood is probably the most despicable. The *Wall Street Journal* once dubbed Planned Parenthood as "Abortion Central" (February 1, 1994). Every year over 227,000 unborn babies are killed by these who traffic in the death of the innocent. Planned Parenthood cloaks itself as reaching out with caring and compassion to pregnant teen girls and women. What they don't tell the victims — and they are victims — is the physical and emotional trauma that they will experience for the rest of their lives.

Planned Parenthood raves about all they have to offer women and girls, but they won't explain the failures. Young women are dying on the tables, hemorrhaging to death. They don't tell you about the ones who develop breast cancer because their bodies are producing milk to feed a baby, a natural physical process that gets interrupted and causes the body to react harshly. They don't advertise the fate of the young women who later regret having destroyed a human life and who commit suicide because they cannot live with the guilt.

Planned Parenthood won't even mention those women and girls who can never get pregnant again even when they want a baby. Their bodies have undergone enough physical damage to their reproductive organs that it is impossible. They certainly won't cite the cases of young women who can't have sex again as a result of the irrational fear that is tied to emotional trauma. Those women go through life feeling like freaks because nobody has explained it. Planned

Parenthood won't be honest about the broken marriages and relationships they have caused by aborting babies without the fathers' knowledge.

Planned Parenthood won't own up to the cases of young women having their insides surgically removed years later because of infection and disease. Planned Parenthood will perform an abortion on a teen girl without notifying her parents. They joined the ACLU in Florida to file a lawsuit to stop legislation that required them to notify parents before an abortion was performed. What kind of people are we dealing with that would seek to hide something so serious and so dangerous from parents? I'll tell you; it is people who understand that parents would intervene and stop it for moral, emotional, spiritual, and physical reasons. Planned Parenthood does not want parents to be involved.

If you are the parent of a female child or teen girl, your reaction has to be, *Who do you think you are to make a decision like that for my child without any input from me. This is my child. How dare you play God in her life?* The disrespect and disdain Planned Parenthood shows toward parents is quite chilling.

Planned Parenthood refused to report a statutory rape in Ohio, thereby violating Ohio's state laws. Planned Parenthood is required by law to notify an underage girl's parents that she is seeking an abortion. In this case, a thirteen-year-old girl was led to have sex with her twenty-one-year-old soccer coach, which resulted in a pregnancy. Once the man found out the girl was pregnant, he took her to an abortion clinic operated by Planned Parenthood and forced her to have an abortion in order to cover up his crime.

Fortunately, the man was found out, arrested, tried, and convicted. He is now in prison. The court said what he did was wrong and a crime, but Planned Parenthood covered it up. This cover-up was not something new for Planned Parenthood. This is their common practice. I pray that one of them goes to prison in this case.

On September 10 of 2003, eighteen-year-old Holly Patterson went to a Planned Parenthood clinic in San Francisco. There she was given the abortion pill RU-486. She followed the prescribed procedure, taking two more pills at home three days later.

She began soon after to experience bleeding and cramps that were so severe she could not walk. Her boyfriend rushed her to the hospital. There she explained what she had done. Painkillers were administered, and she went back home.

Several nights later she was back in the hospital and lay dying in the emergency room from complications that developed after she took the RU-486 abortion pill. Holly Patterson's father was told by the attending physician at the hospital that she had died from a massive infection caused by fragments of the fetus that never left her body. This caused her to go into septic shock.

Holly died because she did not receive appropriate counsel from family or credible physicians, but from Planned Parenthood, who couldn't care less.

This organization long ago crossed the line of civility and continues to flaunt the laws of God and basic respect toward humans. Planned Parenthood does not want you to know that the prime motivation for their existence is money; in fact, millions of dollars.

They receive nearly $400 million every year in tax money. That's right; you and I are helping to foot the bill for this bloody business. Planned Parenthood makes over $810 million a year. That figure is from their own annual reports, surpassing previous records.

Barbarism certainly pays well, doesn't it? But making money has been the goal all along. How despicable is a group that heinously takes the life of an innocent, helpless, and precious baby secure in its mother's womb and ignores the effects on the mother in order to get rich? How wicked do you have to be to develop murder and human suffering into profit and to mine human despair for gold? How vicious are people who will exploit the rights of an innocent girl or a troubled young woman by enticing her to destroy a human life created by God that she can never replace?

Planned Parenthood murders the unborn, traumatizes the mother, and then moves on to the next victim. Cold, callous, and unfeeling, they prey upon a troubled female society full of women who don't understand that two wrongs never make a right, women who are confused and need helpful answers, not destructive outs. That's a wrong solution to a problem of one's own making, and it will only create a host of related problems that will never go away.

Did you ever stop to think about this? Every time a baby is aborted, did they kill the man or woman who would find a cure for cancer or a number of other dreaded diseases? Did they destroy a life that would have had a tremendous positive impact on society for good? Did they prevent the world from knowing a great leader who would have presented a wonderful vision for the future, or a great poet, author, or educator? Planned Parenthood is not only taking the lives of babies and permanently damaging girls and women, but they are killing America's future.

Other nations have become acutely aware of the effects of whole-sale abortion on their future populations. LifeNews.com reported that Russia is offering financial incentives to stem the tide of abnormally high abortion rates. President Vladimir Putin defined the crisis as the nation's biggest problem, and the government is offering hefty bonuses to women to have a second child. The decrease in population numbers were attributed to the nation's high abortion rates.

The age-old question has been asked: is it really murder and not a medical procedure? No, it's not a medical procedure. These girls and women are not sick; they are pregnant. It is a natural process of life, when babies are formed, developing features and feelings.

Partial birth abortion is mankind sinking to the utter depths of inhumanity. Partial means the baby is pulled partially out of the birth canal and killed. If the baby somehow slips out a few more inches and is out completely, and if the attending abortionist (I refuse to call them doctors) kills it, then he has committed murder. So let's beat the system. Let's take life on a technicality and a few inches.

A nurse who worked in an abortion clinic for a day said the following:

> The baby was kicking her feet and whimpering as her life was ruthlessly taken from her. I ran screaming from the building and fell onto the grass outside, sobbing and saying, "Oh God, forgive me for ever walking in that door. What could I have been thinking?" It's not about medical help; it's about a few minutes of torture and murder for money. There is nothing compassionate or caring about it all. I was deceived into believing that I was actually helping someone. But when I looked into the attending doctor's eyes, I saw nothing, and the fear I felt nauseated me.

She told me afterward that having worked in real medicine, "the common thread that linked all those doctors together was respect for life and using their abilities to preserve it, providing real compassion and care for people who were injured or ill." She said, "An abortion clinic has the cold feel of death and evil about it."

No matter how Planned Parenthood advertises itself, no matter how helpful they claim to be, it's just not true. They are sleazy opportunists who profit from the circumstance that careless teens and unthinking women find themselves in. They lure the victims with promises of a quick fix to a complex problem. Planned Parenthood advocates a simple solution to life's greatest occurrence, and that is the conception of new life. They wrongly offer an unacceptable alternative to the acceptance of responsibility for actions taken. They provide an easy out for a careless lifestyle and poor decision making. *Go ahead and do it; if you mess up, we'll take care of it.* They provide an option that is inhumane, an option that should never even be considered when it comes to human life.

Emergency medical personnel, firefighters, police, and rescue workers risk their own lives every single day to rescue people whose lives hang in the balance, making heroic efforts to save just one person's life. Just one person having the privilege to go on living is vitally important to people who are in the lifesaving business. Why? Why do these heroes and heroines take the risk to save another?

Human life is precious. That concept has always been a part of our national psyche. So you see, destroying a baby who cannot defend itself goes against the grain of everything that America was built on.

The high value we as a people place on just one human life, no matter how small, causes us to reverence the sanctity of life, and that separates us from heathens, pagans, and barbarians. While the rest of us are busy trying to preserve life, Planned Parenthood is daily destroying it. Their disturbing attitude was further demonstrated at the Democratic national convention. The leaders were wearing and handing out T-shirts that said, "I had an abortion." What kind of unfeeling, mixed-up women go around advertising that they killed their unborn children? Can you believe it? But you see, this type of behavior is very revealing. It shows the depth of disregard for human life as demonstrated by these radical women.

How far will Planned Parenthood go to flaunt its disdain for life and raise money? Try this. The *National Liberty Journal* reported in its October 2005 issue that on the Planned Parenthood national website, they urged people to donate to hurricane relief; but if you inspected the fine print on that site, the organization explained that all money raised would be used to support its own abortion clinics and offices, not to support any of the rescue efforts or critical services needed by storm victims in New Orleans and along the Gulf Coast.

They exploited the tragedy of Hurricane Katrina for their own financial gain and proved once again that they will stoop to anything to fill their bank account. They clearly demonstrate time and again that they are calculating, callous, and undeserving of any monetary support.

Here was America in the grips of what could be the worst national disaster in history, and all Planned Parenthood could think of was how to get its soiled hands on the money pouring in and earmarked for reserve operations. What further example would anyone need than this to understand what a seedy and vile organization Planned Parenthood really is?

I have spoken to several young women who had abortions, and they told me they find themselves crying a lot even though their abortions happened several years ago. Their bodies, hearts, minds, and consciences just won't allow them to put it away. One said that as the abortion was in progress, she was conscious and overwhelmed with the feeling that what she was doing was awful and she should not do it. That was her humanness telling her, *Don't kill that precious little baby that is a part of you.*

I heard the wrenching story of another young woman who decided at the last possible moment that she had changed her mind and did not want to go through with it. At first the doctor and nurse tried to gently persuade her, but when she still refused, they became angry and verbally abusive, telling her, "You'll have to pay for it anyway." Is this the same organization that advertises itself as caring for women? I believe you would agree it doesn't.

Why does Planned Parenthood involve itself in sex education if its livelihood and existence depend on pregnant teens coming to them for abortions? Well, you see, it's not *responsible* sex education they advocate. It is radical sex education, explicit, pornographic. It's subtly designed to entice teens to have a promiscuous sex life.

Planned Parenthood is distributing a sexually explicit book to children titled *It's Perfectly Normal.* This organization vehemently opposes abstinence education as an ignorant approach to educating teens about sex. They believe that teens should be taught exactly how to have sex and its related pleasures, while at the same time saying their aim is to prevent pregnancies!

You can't put out a forest fire by throwing gasoline on it. It does not take a genius to see how the real intentions are cloaked. Please understand that Planned Parenthood has never had the best interest of any female at heart. It's about a radical feminist agenda and money. *Teach sex so teens will be enticed to have it. Teens get pregnant; tell them when they do, come see us.* That is their philosophy.

Planned Parenthood has partnered with the National Education Association to produce videos and books that literally encourage boys to explore their sexuality with girls.

Again, how despicable is this organization? They actually work to increase teen pregnancy in order to perpetuate the abortion business. We would be incensed if a cardiologist advocated eating five pounds of fat meat every day to drum up business. Equally, we should be incensed that Planned Parenthood promotes a lifestyle among teens that they know will result in teen pregnancies.

Let's try this again. Encourage teens to be promiscuous, so girls will become pregnant, so they will need abortion services. Wow! It is just difficult to comprehend that humans who are supposed to possess some depth of feeling could engage themselves in tactics so loathsome, while at the same time playing Russian roulette with unsuspecting young lives. This is irresponsible citizenship and a reckless exercise of our freedom.

In their continued far-reaching attempts to include everybody in their murder-for-money business, Planned Parenthood has long been seeking to force hospitals, even religious ones, to perform abortions. But according to an article in Lifenews.com, "Congress has approved a law that protects hospitals' health insurance companies and medical professionals who do not want to pay for or perform abortions.

"In December 2004, President Bush signed into law the Hyde-Weldon measure that prohibits agencies that receive federal dollars from discriminating against medical personnel or agencies that do not want to be involved in abortions."

It is about time that government reigned in the ever-extending tentacles of this insidious evil. A nation that will allow the exploitation and murder of the innocent and helpless will soon lose heart for everything else of moral value. We must defend those who cannot defend themselves by exposing Planned Parenthood. Fathers and mothers should use every respectful and legal means of dissent at their disposal to protect their daughters and to educate the general public about this scourge called abortion before it eats away our conscience like a spreading cancer. We must defend the innocent and helpless lest we suffer the same fate when we are old and deemed useless. We will reap what we sow.

We must collectively summon the courage to stand and proclaim the truth about murder and deception cloaked as compassion.

Chapter 14

Judicial Tyranny

Cloaked as Justice

—ɷ—

Webster's New World Dictionary defines a tyrant as "an absolute ruler and oppressive." Tyranny is defined as an unjust use of power. That aptly describes a rebel group of judiciary in America. They are tyrants of the United States system of justice, judges who have elevated themselves from agents of justice to tyrants who play fast and loose with the law, rendering decisions that oppress the will of the majority of the American people.

Voters elect lawmakers, commissioning them to pass laws that reflect the majority opinion of the nation or the state. That is government of the people, by, and for the people. Tyrannical judges, on the other hand, have usurped the laws of the land in order to impose not an opinion of the law, but in most cases disregard of the law altogether. Some even assume to violate the law themselves, as one judge did in New York when she escorted a criminal out the back door of the courthouse to help him avoid capture. Why? She didn't agree with the charges brought against him. By the way, no legal action was taken against her.

Americans have had it with judges sending down decisions that reflect their own will instead of the law. This is absolute ruler mentality. In other words, corrupt judges (and this type of behavior is corrupt) believe their position gives them the power to decide what is equitable for the rest of us with no regard for the law. The law is routinely usurped in favor of personal view. The law many times is not interpreted or given consideration by these judges. The law is bypassed entirely in the formation of radical rulings.

Worst of all, these pious judicial outlaws pervert the true intent of the framers of our Constitution and our founding fathers. They have become the new self-appointed framers of the Constitution and the new founding fathers and authors of the law, foisting on America an unheard of jurisprudence and thereby bringing a new and dangerous mind-set to the judiciary. This mind-set translates into an open license to render law moot and replace it with liberal judicial opinion derived from years of social brainwashing.

These opinions frustrate both lawmakers and the millions of people who fall victim to these horrendous verdicts. These verdicts are illogical and unhistorical, overruling laws that have served our society successfully for over two hundred years. They interpret to suit their own agendas, casting aside juridical protocol. Taking these types of careless liberties with the justice system results in verdicts that are oppressive to people and unsound for the well-being of our nation as a whole.

Where did we go wrong with our judiciary? Here's where! As a people, we have given too much power to judges by allowing them to serve on the Supreme Court and appeals courts for life. We have allowed judges to wield power unchecked, from the local magistrate all the way to the Supreme Court. We have ignored judicial corruption, while capitulating to those who hold authority and not challenging their behavior. We are partly to blame for allowing judges to exalt themselves to supreme authority over us, rather than serving us. That gift of perceived power has given many the impression that they are infallible and even reside above the law.

I submit, the justices on the Supreme Court have become supremacist. They actually believe in the absolute supremacy of their own group. Judicial power has served as a mental stimulant that causes some to think more highly of themselves than actuality would permit. This court needs to be reminded often that *supreme* means highest rank, nothing more. The Supreme Court is the final court of appeal, not the supreme justice of the universe. That belongs to God. Somebody needs to humble this court with that fact.

Since I was about twenty years old, I have observed and noted the corruption of judges—from the local magistrate who winked at the wife beater, dropped the charges, and told the wife (whose face was puffy from blows to the head) to go home and behave and get along with her husband, to a circuit judge who dismissed drunken-driving charges against a man who struck two little girls on bicycles with his car and killed them both, ruling it was an accident. I have seen family court judges cut backroom deals and award custody of children to a parent who was totally unfit, or give every other weekend unsupervised visitation rights to a drug dealer or a prostitute.

State supreme court justices, once they arrive on the bench, protect unscrupulous lawyers, leaving the general public with no recourse for justice. One state supreme court justice left a party drunk, and while driving home, she struck a parked car but did not stop until she was home. When the police arrived, she was not arrested. She simply paid a fine, after outrage and a public outcry. You and I would have been in jail facing multiple charges. She was deferred to because she was a state supreme court justice.

We as a people need to collectively rise up and remind judges that they are not overlords or demigods, but servants of the people who serve justly at the will of the people. Benjamin Franklin said, "Rebellion to tyrants is obedience to God." All public officials should be held accountable for their actions.

Politicians and businesspeople also bear a portion of the responsibility for judicial malpractice. Judges are afforded monarch status at public events. They receive too much recognition that artificially exalts. The term *Your Honor* used to mean something, and it still does to some, while calling others Your Honor is a misnomer, for they possess no honor and deserve none.

Former president Jimmy Carter is also responsible for a major portion of the problems with our national judiciary. In his four years in office, Carter appointed some of the most liberal appeals court justices than did any other president. He will always be remembered as the father of modern-day liberalism. It's difficult to say this about a former president, but Carter was an ignorant man who was convinced that to find his place in history, he had to balance the judiciary with a goodly number of liberals. Those who yell and scream and curse biased judicial ruling are the same people who voted for Bill Clinton twice. Clinton thanked them by appointing radical judges to any position available for him to fill.

We as Americans have fed the judiciary; now it has become a monster that threatens to devour the laws of the land and the Constitution, a document that has fortified us as a nation. Rogue judges have allowed the ACLU to abuse the federal courts and use the courts as a weapon to turn America into an atheist nation. Whose side are they on? Certainly not mine and yours! If we sit idly by and don't become proactive, this relentless attack on America will leave the Constitution shredded at our feet, forcing us to live by a judicial sway that will destroy all sense of justice in the courts and deny the will of the majority of America.

In Massachusetts the outlaw supreme court there blatantly dictated legal precedent to the legislature concerning gay marriage.

Legislators, who were elected by the people to pass laws reflective of that state's community standards and moral convictions, had voted to ban gay marriage. They were overruled by a flagrant judicial coup.

If judicial dictators can overrule lawmakers, why are elections even necessary? That's a sham! Judicial activists are fast becoming an overriding force in America. If this trend continues, we will be a government and a people that suffer at the whim of judges who are, for the most part, left-wingers and legal bomb throwers.

Again and again we see judges in almost every state in the Union defying standing laws and mocking both justice and the fair judgment desire of the populace. Judge Larry Meyer, a Missouri circuit court judge, gave Kenneth Slaught probation for raping a nine-year-old girl, but no prison time.

This outlaw judge is practicing "restorative justice." He has bought in to the secular progressive idea that the rapist and child molester need to be restored to society. To do what? Rape another child. This judge has no moral conscience and no understanding of the relation of crime to proper punishment.

Judge Edward Cashman of Vermont District Court sentenced Mark Holett to sixty days for raping both a six-year-old and a ten-year-old girl. The prosecutor pleaded for a twenty-year sentence. To any person with a sense of justice, the sentence was heinous.

Judges who render this type of justice are ensuring that these perverts will be able to continue destroying children. When pressed on the issue, Judge Cashman said, "That punishment would be too harsh." Excuse me! The last time I looked, punishment was legal in the United States. This is an activist judge, a left-wing radical jurist who has gone completely over the cliff.

One man burned his wife and child to death in a house fire, allegedly to collect $345,000 in insurance. The judge presiding over the case freed him because he said the prosecutor had delayed the trial.

Matthew Staver, reporting in the *Liberty Journal* gives an account of Ninth U.S. Court of Appeals Judge Stephen Reinhardt, who ruled that parental rights to direct the upbringing of their children are immobilized at the "threshold of the school door." If you are looking for a judge who is ignorant of both the law and civil rights, here he is!

The parents had filed suit to stop the school from giving their seven-year-old a sex questionnaire. The judge said that the parents surrendered their God-given rights over their children to the public school. He further stated that "parents are not the exclusive providers of information regarding sexual matters to their children" and that "parents have no due process of privacy right to override the select determinations of public schools as to the information to which their children will be exposed."

In other words, your children are not yours; they belong to government and the government-approved school system. If we as Americans don't rise up in arms over this type of judicial dictatorship, we will lose the future of our children.

Just remember: God gave your children to you, and you should have the right to safeguard them from information that will harm and confuse their young minds.

This type of indoctrination is akin to mental rape. The survey asked the children how often they touched their private parts. Did they think about having sex? Did they think about touching other people's private parts? Did they sometimes get scared when thinking about sex? Did they have times when they couldn't stop thinking about sex?

These are seven-year-olds having their innocent minds violated with filthy thoughts. They should be thinking about recess and lunch and reading a book. We as adults must wake up and take a stand.

The United States Ninth Circuit Court of Appeals in California ruled that the Pledge of Allegiance should not be allowed in schools. Why not? It contained the words *one nation under God*. In reality this court was simply furthering the rantings of a radical atheist. What about the rest of the people in California? These judicial pirates don't care. I can't say that too many times. *They don't care!*

This left-leaning court is a picture-perfect example of how law-usurping, anti-God and anti-American judges are becoming bolder and more aggressive toward long-held principles and laws that embody America. It's obvious we have not been diligent in keeping our campfires burning against the rogue judiciary, and now these legal wolves are drawing ever closer to us. Make no mistake; if left unchecked, these liberal activists cloaked in robes that signify justice will dismantle every single existing law they disagree with.

The detriment to states individually and the nation as a whole will be catastrophic.

The Colorado Supreme Court threw out a rape and murder conviction because a juror consulted the Bible during deliberations! The defense attorneys, grasping for any straw that would save their heartless client's behind, argued that "the jury had gone outside of the law when they went to the Bible to seek God's position on capital punishment," and this liberal court agreed.

To release a killer on such a thin argument is insane. What of the rights of the woman who was raped and whose life was ruthlessly taken? Obviously, she didn't deserve justice, according to them. It's rulings like this that sicken and anger the populace.

The supreme court in the state of Florida, made up of rank liberal Democrats, ruled time and again for Al Gore in the vote-counting debacle. If this court had possessed one ounce of integrity, that election would have ended quickly. Instead, they chose to use their position on the bench to benefit their own political party, prolonging an issue that should have swiftly died.

Is that fair representation and justice for the Republicans in the state of Florida? No, it is not! But try telling that to these tyrants in black robes who twisted and wrested the law from its design and purpose.

In an attempt to fashion a win for Al Gore, this court may go down in history as displaying the most outright disdain of justice in favor of personal ideology of any court to date. They did so while exhibiting bad attitudes and scowling faces as they held court. If this sorry bunch did not reveal to all of America the type of thinking that has come to be commonplace with social agenda judges, I cannot imagine what would. Their lack of fairness cost millions and millions of dollars to the state of Florida and to both Bush and Gore. By the way, they dismissed accusations that thousands of New York Democrats voted absentee in New York and came to their vacation homes in Florida and voted again. This was later proven.

We must recognize the immediate danger to our system of justice when we have judges of this ilk sitting on influential benches all over America. As Dick Scarborough said in *Vision America,* "The American people are patient, law-abiding, and long-suffering, but time is running out. If we don't act soon, we may not have a country left to save. Fidelity to the Constitution requires rejection of the unlawful edicts of judicial autocrats."

He is right, and rejection is the course of action America needs to take. Article III, Section 1 of the U.S. Constitution declares, "Judges both of supreme and inferior courts shall hold their offices during good behavior." The defiant actions of judges and the decisions being handed down now could never qualify as good behavior. This provision gives Congress the power to remove from the bench those justices who flaunt the Constitution and state law.

The American people are the victims, and we need to rise up and demand that Congress take the appropriate action before these left-leaning liberals eradicate existing laws, throw our country into peril, and perpetrate biased evil throughout our society.

Article III, Section 2 of the U.S Constitution provides for legislative bodies to carefully define and restrict the far-reaching boundaries of federal courts, confining judges to lesser areas of judicial oversight and control. For example, an appeals court in Virginia can tell a small town council in upper South Carolina that they can no longer open their sessions with prayer. Why? It is because a practicing witch was offended. This type of far-ranging judicial ruling needs to be stopped in favor of more localized judicial decisions by judges who reflect local opinion and whose state senators and congressmen have had an influence in placing them on the bench. This attack on America by socially brainwashed judges is akin to a runaway semitruck in heavy traffic. If we don't stop it soon, there will be casualties all over the place.

We need men and women of character, integrity, and loyalty to the letter of the law to sit in legal judgment of America, justices we can trust to honor and respect law and not pervert it or overshadow its clear meanings, and jurists who understand and accept the will of the people. We are a nation that chooses how we will live and what laws will govern us.

That is a sacred principle of American life that must never be tampered with. To do so would upset the delicate balance that has provided us protection, security, and justice. We must be vigilant about calling in to account those who would accomplish by judicial fiat what they cannot change through the electoral and law-making process.

Using the free speech argument, the United States Supreme Court blocked a law proposed to guard children who use the Internet from pornographic sites. It did not matter that some boy may become a rapist or act out on a younger child what he saw on the Internet. Let's not hinder the free speech rights of porn-seeking adults who surf the Net searching for a cheap, tawdry thrill. That is insanity! Let's just provide the elements that will destroy the decency of future generations in order to placate the perverted appetites of weirdos. Has the court lost all reason?

Now remember, according to the Supreme Court, indecent material is protected by the First Amendment. That's pushing the envelope to the extreme. Adults have the right to purchase the objectionable material, but children may not. Well, what provision has this court made to enforce the rule that prohibits children from viewing it? I'll tell you — none! In the name of free speech, let's saturate the minds of innocent children with filth and create future sexual predators and monsters. That is the type of judicial irresponsibility that will kill our nation if these legal gods for life hold hostage the people in America who believe the shield law should have been put into effect.

Has the complexion of the Supreme Court changed in regard to recent decisions? Has the Court abandoned correct rulings for corrupt ones? Yes! Seventeen years ago the Supreme Court upheld sodomy laws but recently departed from that long-held position with a ruling that declared sodomy a "right" of those who want to practice it. What happened? What was repulsive seventeen years ago still is today.

The most appalling thing about judicial decisions such as this is the fact that the overwhelming majority has to bear the brunt in order to provide so-called rights to a very small minority of creeps, idiots, atheists, liberals, socialists, terrorists, traitors, and social-change fanatics. That is not the way democracy was intended to function. Courts have extended beyond their authority, virtually ignoring the desires of America for a few disgruntled people who will never be pleased. That is tyranny! When minority belief, whether of one or a few, is imposed over the objection of the majority, that is a tyrannical position to take.

Activist courts have abandoned principle, seizing the opportunity to impose a radical agenda. A district court judge in San Francisco, who personally and vocally advocated any abortion procedure and is militant about his position believing it to be a woman's right to kill, overruled the government mandated ban on partial birth abortion signed by the President of the United States. Driven by his personal opinion, he actually violated the law himself. That makes him a judicial charlatan who cannot and should not be trusted. A true judge is one who renders a judgment based on the law—*period*.

During the Republican national convention in New York City, protestors, including socialists, anti-Americans, Bush-haters, and those who want to overthrow the U.S. government marched and congregated in the streets outside Madison Square Garden. People feared for their safety as many protestors turned unruly and violent. One protester stomped a police officer in the head after the officer had fallen to the pavement in a crowd surge. Many were arrested for violating peaceful protest laws.

Now get this; a Far Left-leaning judge fined the city of New York one thousand dollars for every protester arrested. He must be reliving his days at Woodstock. Can you believe it? The fact that this bonehead is sitting on a judicial bench has to be frightening to the police and the citizens of New York.

There should be an instant outcry at this in-your-face jurist. A ruling so anti-establishment and so outrageous clearly demonstrates yet again that judges such as this one have no shame when it pertains to imposing their own liberal prejudices at the expense of people and the law.

I would be remiss if I did not praise the judges in America who do stand firm on the law. There are judges who impose sentences according to the law and the crime, using common sense compassion and a firm intolerance of criminal behavior, judges who still believe the adage "You do the crime, you do the time."

One such Judge is William Young, 12th U.S. District Court. If you recall, he is the judge who sentenced Richard Reid, the terrorist who boarded an airplane with a homemade explosive device in his shoe that he was going to use to blow up the plane in midair. Reid was thwarted in his attempt to light it. He was subsequently arrested and tried. Before he was sentenced, after admitting guilt and his unwavering "allegiance to Osama bin Laden, to Islam, and to the religion of Allah," Reid was defiant in saying, "I think I will not apologize for my actions." He told the judge, "I am at war with your country."

After pronouncing his sentence, a sentence of life in prison, Judge Young said this:

> This is the sentence that is provided for by our statutes. It is a fair and just sentence. It is a righteous sentence.

Now, let me explain this to you. We are not afraid of you or any of your terrorist co-conspirators, Mr. Reid. We are Americans. We have been through the fire before. There is too much war talk here, and I say that to everyone with the utmost respect. Here in this court, we deal with individuals as individuals and care for individuals as individuals. As human beings, we reach out for justice.

You are not an enemy combatant. You are a terrorist. You are not a soldier in any war. You are a terrorist. To give you that reference, to call you a soldier, gives you far too much stature. Whether the officers of government do it or your attorney does it, or if you think you are a soldier. You are not. . . . You are a terrorist. And we do not negotiate with terrorists. We do not meet with terrorists. We do not sign documents with terrorists. We hunt them down one by one and bring them to justice.

So war talk is way out of line in this court. You are a big fellow. But you are not that big. You're no warrior. I've known warriors. You are a terrorist: a species of criminal that is guilty of multiple attempted murders. In a very real sense, State Trooper Santiago had it right when you first were taken off that plane and into custody and you wondered where the press and the TV crew were, and he said, "You're no big deal." *You **are** no big deal.*

What your able counsel and what the equally able United States attorneys have grappled with and what I have as honestly as I know how tried to grapple with is why you did something so horrific. What was it that led you here to this courtroom today?

I have listened respectfully to what you have to say. And I ask you to search your heart and ask yourself what sort of unfathomable hate led you to do what you are guilty and admit you are guilty of doing? And, I have an answer for you. It may not satisfy you, but as I search this entire record, it comes as close to understanding as I know.

It seems to me you hate the one thing that to us is most precious. You hate our freedom, our individual freedom. Our individual freedom is to live as we choose, to come and go as we choose, to believe or not believe as we individually choose. Here, in this society, the very wind carries freedom. It carries it everywhere from sea to shining sea.

It is because we prize individual freedom so much that you are here in this beautiful courtroom. So that everyone can see, truly see, that justice is administered fairly, individually, and discreetly. It is for freedom's sake that your lawyers are striving so vigorously on your behalf, have filed appeals, will go on in their representation of you before other judges.

We Americans are all about freedom. Because we all know that the way we treat you, Mr. Reid, is the measure of our own liberties. Make no mistake though. It is yet true that we will bear any burden, pay any price, to preserve our freedoms. Look around this courtroom. Mark it well. The world is not going to long remember what you or I say here. The day after tomorrow, it will be forgotten; but this, however, will long endure.

Here in this courtroom and courtrooms all across America, the American people will gather to see that justice, individual justice, justice, not war, individual justice is in fact being done. The very President of the United States through his officers will have to come into courtrooms and lay out evidence on which specific matters can be judged, and juries of citizens will gather to sit and judge that evidence democratically, to mold and shape and refine our sense of justice.

See that flag, Mr. Reid? That's the flag of the United States of America. That flag will fly there long after this is all forgotten. That flag stands for freedom. And it always will.

Mr. Custody Officer, stand him down.

Anti-Christian judges have fallen on Christians like lions on help-less gazelles, using judicial powers to add words to the Constitution in order to remove Christianity's influence from public life. In 1844 the United States Supreme Court ruled in a unanimous opinion that "Christianity . . . is not to be maliciously and openly reviled and blasphemed against, to the annoyance of believers of the injury of the public." Atheist judges are enabling radical groups to extermi-nate Christianity through their courts, fully aware they could not win in the court of public opinion. These Christian-bashers retreat to the halls of justice where justice is not to be found for Christianity.

Judicial tyrants, cloaked as judges who are trusted by the people to mete out justice fair and sound, are flagrantly violating that trust and imposing by court edict a standard of conduct that encourages a further decadence in our society. This is a license to commit evil in a way which we have never experienced in our nation's history.

America's moral laws are being replaced by foul judicial fiat that will surely result in a severe weakening of our mode of justice. When that happens, we will become an unprincipled, unguided, lawless, immoral, and godless nation. We will die, stripped of sustaining laws. With these judicial tyrants on benches across this country, it is no wonder our symbol of justice is blindfolded—she can't bear to look.

Chapter 15

Flooding America with Illegal Aliens

Cloaked in an Open-Border Mentality

—ᨆ—

I have heard all the noble and sympathetic-sounding arguments and all the flimsy reasons for opening our borders to the teeming masses. These arguments are drawn from the past history of immigration. This was a time when people from other countries wanted to breathe the fresh air of freedom. These people possessed a burning desire in their souls for a better life through the wonderful new opportunities that America offered.

The present population in our nation consists of descendants from those pioneer immigrants. But the difference between the immigrants of the past and those of today is stark, and the contrast is disturbing and even frightening to some. The immigrants who sought refuge in America years ago really wanted to be Americans.

They were glad to incorporate themselves into everything that made America great. They wanted to embrace our culture, our God, our governance, and our society. They wanted desperately to learn our language, salute our flag, sing our national anthem, fight for our country, and volunteer where needed.

They had pride. They wanted to work. Lying on their backsides and doing nothing was a disgrace. They knew that American ideals and values were carved out over decades of trial and error, tears and laughter, peace and war, failure and success. But they knew that America at its worst offered a brighter promise of a better life than the places they came from.

Many brought with them ingenuity, talents, and abilities that contributed to the overall quality of life. Those immigrants of yesterday truly made America their new home, and Americans became their countrymen.

Immigrants today are far removed from those of our past. Most, but *not all,* have entered this country illegally; some have entered to kill our citizens and wreak havoc on our economy. Others have come to slowly and ever so subtly take over America through religious lunacy.

Upon arriving here, many immigrants immediately begin to seek all the free government giveaways they can find, and of course, they are encouraged by "give America away" idiots who worship at the altar of entitlements. Most of this new strain of immigrants wants to force America to cater to their dislikes of American life.

They have blatantly demonstrated their unwillingness to adapt to our laws, our culture, and our system of government. They yell and protest that we are offending them. They are not for America. They are not patriots. They are, in fact, anti-American, and they proved it at the United States versus Mexico soccer game at the Los Angeles Coliseum. The crowd was predominantly Mexican, but living in the United States; yet you would have never known it as they booed during the national anthem and turned American flags upside down.

To add more insult, as the game went on, the U.S. players had obscenities yelled at them, and objects were thrown; some players were even punched and spat upon as the game ended. These people are not U.S. citizens; they are foreign devils who should be driven out of California and out of this country.

I have found that those who sneak across our borders also have no sense of honest responsibility. They learn fast which politicians will take care of their every need. There are many liberals and secular progressives who are happy to oblige, even though the federal government spends over sixty billion dollars a year on immigration-related costs. Thousands are given free education, money, rooms, and food.

Most of these modern-day immigrants are not seeking opportunity; they are seeking an opening to exploit every single program that was put into place to help Americans who truly need assistance and who deserve it. Somehow, aliens, illegal and otherwise, have come to the conclusion that they should be more privileged than the rest of us. But we are not obligated to dole out no-interest loans, tax breaks, free housing, and transportation, or give unlimited incentives.

Now, I believe that America should remain a place of opportunity and education to an individual who has the same designs on America as the pioneer immigrants. But, I say if you don't respect America and its people, then don't come here, because the majority of us do respect our country and are not interested in changing to suit your whiny, unreasonable demands.

We are not going to stand idly by and let you wreck what so many have toiled and even died to preserve. You can call us bigots, racists, or whatever else you might want to say, but harsh rhetoric will not bully us into submitting to your loud and boisterous, disrespectful mouths.

The true American people, the real honest-to-God lovers of this country are still proud to be Americans. We refuse to feel guilty about our prosperity, our accomplishments, our wealth, our technology, or your predicament. Let me say it another way. If you did not come to America with a humble spirit, a grateful heart, and a deep appreciation for the opportunity that you will have to change your life for the better, then I suggest that you turn right around and go back to where you came from.

We must wake up! America can no longer ignore the massive flood of illegals into our country, over twelve million in California alone. In the county of Los Angeles, it has been reported that over four hundred thousand illegals are living in garages provided by other aliens.

Our welfare system, hospitals, health care, and housing programs are being severely overloaded by the sheer numbers. It has been estimated by the federal government that 41 percent of HUD projects are occupied by illegals. This is a staggering statistic. Check out the HUD reports.

The overwhelming task of trying to appease, placate, feed, and educate millions of illegals is already beginning to drain our resources. Because remember, most don't put anything back into the economy. Some of the ones who are gainfully employed get their paychecks and send them back home to family, so it's never invested in America's economy.

If this trend continues, economic chaos and ruin will follow as illegals clamor to extract even more from a government that has nothing left to give. Then riots will start in major cities, looting and killing. The fastest growing gangs in America and the most dangerous are illegal aliens. Police don't have databases, names, fingerprints, or identification that will aid in catching them. Illegal aliens, driving drunk, have been responsible for a number of deaths. *[Fox News]* When those accidents happen, the driver has no driver's license or insurance, and most times local police can't or won't file charges. This leaves the victims helpless to recoup loses for injuries or damages. So illegals commit more and more violent crimes and become bolder about it.

We must pass meaningful immigration laws. These laws should be rock solid so they cannot be dismantled by unscrupulous lawyers. All politicians in Washington must recognize that unity on this issue has to be achieved. Time is running out.

Open borders are not an option now or ever because of not only the dangers involved, but also the debilitating effect it will have on an already overtaxed populace. Strong measures must be taken, even if it means deporting every illegal alien back to his or her own country.

For the future of America, it has to be done. Those politicians who don't have the stomach for the fight need to resign. Americans are tired of being represented by wimps and slackers. We need real men and women who put America first and everybody else second.

The threat that unchecked illegal immigration brings to America is best described by Dick Lamm, former governor of Colorado. Governor Lamm spoke at an immigration overpopulation conference in Washington, D.C. He was the keynote speaker and was preceded at the podium by Victor Davis, author of the book *Mexifornia*. The gist of this book is how rampant immigration is taking over California and how it will soon take over the entire nation.

After Mr. Davis's speech ended, former governor Lamm delivered an eloquent and mind-numbing speech, describing in detail what it will take to destroy America. Here is what he said:

> If you believe that America is too smug, too self-satisfied, too rich, then let's destroy America. It is not that hard to do. No nation in history has survived the ravages of time. Arnold Toynbee observed that all great civilizations rise and fall and that "an autopsy of history would show that all great nations commit suicide."
>
> Here is how they do it. *First,* to destroy America, turn America into a bilingual or multilingual, and bicultural country. History shows that no nation can survive the tension, conflict, and antagonism of two or more competing languages and cultures. It is a blessing for an individual to be bilingual; however, it is a curse for a society to be bilingual. The historical scholar Seymour Lipset put it this way: "The histories of turmoil, tension,

and tragedy. Canada, Belgium, Malaysia, and Lebanon all face crises of national existence in which minorities press for autonomy, if not independence. Pakistan and Cyprus have divided. Nigeria suppressed an ethnic rebellion. France faces difficulties with Basques, Bretons, and Corsicans."

Second, to destroy America, invent multiculturalism and encourage immigrants to maintain their culture. I would make it an article of belief that all cultures are equal. That there are no cultural differences. I would make it an article of faith that the black and Hispanic dropout rates are due solely to prejudice and discrimination by the majority. Every other explanation is out of bounds.

Third, we could make the United States an Hispanic Quebec without much effort. The key is to celebrate diversity rather than unity. As Benjamin Schwarz said in the *Atlantic Monthly* recently: "The apparent success of our own multiethnic and multicultural experiment might have been achieved not by tolerance but by hegemony. Without the dominance that once dictated ethnocentricity and what it meant to be an American, we are left with only tolerance and pluralism to hold us together." I would encourage all immigrants to keep their own language and culture. I would replace the melting-pot metaphor with the salad-bowl metaphor. It is important to ensure that we have various cultural subgroups living in America enforcing their differences, rather than as Americans emphasizing their similarities.

Fourth, I would make our fastest growing demographic group the least educated. I would add a second underclass, unassimilated, undereducated, and antagonistic to our population. I would have this second underclass have a 50 percent dropout rate from high school.

My *fifth* point for destroying America would be to get big foundations and business to give these efforts lots of money. I would invest in ethnic identity, and I would establish a cult of "victimology." I would get all minorities to think that their lack of success was the fault of the majority. I would start a grievance industry blaming all minority failure on the majority population.

My *sixth* plan for America's downfall would include dual citizenship and promote divided loyalties. I would celebrate diversity over unity. I would stress differences rather than similarities. Diverse people worldwide are mostly engaged in hating each other—that is, when they are not killing each other. A diverse, peaceful, or stable society is against most historical precedents. People undervalue the unity it takes to keep a nation together. Look at the ancient Greeks. The Greeks believed that they belonged to the same race; they possessed a common language and literature; and they worshipped the same gods. All Greece took part in the Olympic Games. A common enemy, Persia, threatened their liberty. Yet all these bonds were not strong enough to overcome two factors: local patriotism and geographical conditions that nurtured political divisions. Greece fell. *E pluribus unum*—"From many, one." In that historical reality, if we put the emphasis on the *pluribus* instead of the *unum*, we will balkanize America as surely as Kosovo.

Next to last, I would place all subjects off limits; make it taboo to talk about anything against the cult of diversity. I would find a word similar to *heretic* in the sixteenth century that stopped discussion and paralyzed thinking. Words like *racist* or *xenophobe* halt discussion and debate. Having made America a bilingual-bicultural country, having established multiculturalism, having the large foundations fund the doctrine of victimology, I would next make it impossible to enforce our immigration laws.

I would develop a mantra: that because immigration has been good for America, it must always be good. I would make every individual immigrant symmetric and ignore the cumulative impact of millions of them.

Lastly, I would censor Victor Hanson Davis's book *Mexifornia.* His book is dangerous. It exposes the plan to destroy America. If you feel America *deserves* to be destroyed, *don't read this book.*

Unfortunately, we are already experiencing the brutal reality of this alarming but courageous speech. Just look around at how our way of life has already been altered by a persuasive advance of multiple cultures, some whose lifestyles are totally pagan in nature.

Our nation is at a precipice and being pushed hard toward a fall from which there will be no recovery. If we cave in to the unsound reasoning of open-borders proponents, then America's cities will not be a melting pot, but a boiling pot flooded with illegal aliens of every mind-set that you could imagine, and we will drown in a sea of human despair.

Chapter 16

Predatory Lenders

Cloaked as Responsible Loan Companies

B y definition the word *predatory,* according to *Webster's Dictionary,* means "inclined or intended to injure or exploit others as personal gain or profit." Loan companies throughout the country that provide high-interest loans to desperate people are by definition predatory lenders. Predatory lending is practiced not only by companies that loan money, but also by companies that provide credit cards to consumers to buy their products. Then they impose credit card late fees that can go all the way up to 29 percent.

Some credit card companies have been caught holding payments and telling the cardholder that the payment arrived after the due date. Then they raise the interest rates to the maximum allowed in that particular state. That is legalized loan-sharking, fraud, and it has to be a violation of the Unfair Trade Practices Act.

Yes, it is hard to believe, but true. This has to be one of the worst and most despicable things you can do to your fellow man, for a company to deliberately hold an on-time payment and lie about it in order to justify gouging people financially.

Here is a scenario. A young couple with kids buys some furniture on a major store's credit card. Through circumstances beyond their control, a couple of months later they send their fifty-dollar payment a few days beyond the past due date. So what does the company do to accommodate this young couple who shopped with them and who is struggling to pay the fifty-dollar payment on time? They punish them by raising the interest rate from 12 percent to 24.

How stupid is that? Common sense would tell you that if the couple cannot pay fifty dollars, how in the world are they going to pay even more? But you see, these companies don't care. You are trapped, and they will ruin your credit if you don't pay the high interest payment.

This is the standard method of operation for these predatory lenders. They have no conscience at all and no loyalty to the customer, just greed and avarice.

Yes, people should avoid companies that do business this way. They hook people by sending out letters to naïve consumers, offering 6 percent interest for six months or a year; then they raise it to 12 percent if you are fortunate to make it the six months.

The fine print that most never read says these lenders can raise the interest rate at any time they want for any or no reason. That fact alone should scare the daylights out of people, but it won't. And predatory lenders know it. How do they know it? A large percentage of Americans have demonstrated poor financial decision making.

The attitude of borrowing is best described this way: people spend money they don't have in order to buy things that they don't need to impress people they don't like. I have heard financially strapped people actually say, "I want it right now even though I know I cannot afford it." When millions of people think this way, predatory lenders have a willing market to prey upon.

Payday lending is yet another form of predatory lending. Here is how it works: You take out a loan until your next payday. The interest rates can triple and quadruple. The problem comes when your next payday rolls around and you can't come up with the money. So you go back to the payday lender, roll the loan over, and add the payment and the fees to it. Now it is almost doubled, and next payday, if your financial situation prevents you from paying the loan, you go back to the payday lender again. You can easily see where this is headed.

The Center for Responsible Lending in Durham, North Carolina, studied payday lending and discovered that second- and third-time borrowers accounted for 91 percent of the income to payday lenders. The study also found that some of those who borrow do so up to thirteen times in a year. Payday lending makes destructive behavior easy.

They also found that a borrower may pay back $1,000 for a $450 loan. That is absolutely horrible. The study further revealed that 75 percent of payday lending income is derived from the fees exacted from borrowers who are imprisoned by a huge debt load.

This type of irresponsible lending practice, coupled with uninformed borrowers, will most certainly drop these victims into an abyss from which they may never return.

It has been calculated in some states that payday lending interest rates have topped 390 percent. In a civilized and modern society of laws and acceptable business practices, this is unthinkable.

Payday lending is never a long-term solution. It is instead a temporary financial fix akin to putting a Band-Aid on melanoma skin cancer. It simply will not cure the problem, only prolong the serious reality of mismanaged finances and reckless spending habits; and the problem worsens.

Thankfully, some help is being offered. The Federal Deposit Insurance Corporation has encouraged the banking industry to develop and offer lending products that will meet the special needs of people who feel that payday lending is their only hope. In other words, offer legitimate alternatives to financial seductions.

Many wonder how payday lenders are surviving, especially when so many people in the financial field see it as a vice. Here's the answer! In some states, the payday lending industry is backed by too many fat-cat politicians who would rather have their perks than protect the general public. Payday-lending interest rates in some states have climbed to the unimaginable height of 1,000 percent. What in the world can we Americans be thinking to allow this to happen to despairing people who just happen to have no one else to turn to?

One of the most well-known payday lenders is Advance America Cash Advance. In an article in the August 6, 2007, *Post and Courier,* writer Peter Hull said this: "A Pennsylvania court has ruled that Advance America violated consumer law in that state. The court agreed with the state's banking department's claim that fees charged by Advance America exceeded limits of the state's Consumer Discount Company Act. The banking department sued Advance America, alleging that they were providing lines of credit without a license and with interest and fees in excess of state law."

More local action like that taken by Pennsylvania needs to be taken by other states. Some states, such as North Carolina and Georgia, have outright banned payday lending, and they are to be commended.

Title loans are yet another form of predatory lending. People who are in dire need of money go to these lenders, and in exchange for their car title, the lender loans the borrower money. The lender then holds the title until the high-interest loan is paid in full according to the terms.

This is scary, because if the borrower, who is obviously already experiencing financial difficulty, defaults on the payment, the car then belongs to the lender. As you can see, a financially strapped person is now without transportation to go to work and make the money necessary to recoup the car or to provide for his or her family.

Many predatory lenders set up shop in poor neighborhoods where people are uneducated about loan contracts. They just don't realize how foolish it can be to enter into risky agreements like these.

Rent-to-own companies get in on the action as well, charging interest rates that skyrocket if bills are paid late. By the time you pay for the furniture, if you do, you are likely to own cheap junk.

Pentagon leaders have requested that Congress take immediate action to protect gullible military personnel from predatory lenders. You can sometimes find multiple predatory lenders just outside the gates of military bases. The hook is to give soldiers the impression that payday lending is sanctioned by armed forces leadership, but nothing could be further from the truth.

The request to Congress was backed up by the Department of Defense report that predatory lending is threatening vital military standards of conduct and adversely affecting the families of military personnel. Depression is becoming a major problem for those who are deep in debt to payday lenders, those who are trapped and see no way out. The rigors of military life are demanding enough on those who serve; the added worry of massive unpaid debt can sometimes push a man or woman over the edge.

Divorce is another reality for those who have carelessly jeopardized their family's security, and most have done so without even realizing it until it was too late. No wonder the military brass is concerned. A military man or woman cannot function when his or her personal life is falling apart.

If serious problems like these were a direct result of military service, it might be understandable; but they are not related to serving. They are caused by predatory lending companies that seize a needy circumstance and then capture a man or woman into financial bondage. One military sergeant borrowed five hundred dollars from a payday lender, and the interest rates rose and compounded each time she renewed the loan in order to pay the previous note. She suddenly found herself drowning in nearly thirteen thousand dollars of debt.

Most of these victims had to seek counsel from the military. As these incidents were documented, military leaders noticed a pattern of financial abuse. The sheer number of military personnel who were in serious debt was staggering. The Pentagon was compelled to request that Congress take action to end the abuse. To their credit, Congress passed a law that established a lending cap of 36 percent interest on all loans made to the military. President Bush then signed the bill into law.

This was a prudent move. Military life is demanding at best and very stressful at worst. We need to protect our nation's fighting force and ensure that they are treated fairly. Every state needs to follow suit and protect its citizens, especially those who prove to make bad financial judgments.

As a civilized society, we must not allow the vulnerable among us to be picked off one by one by an enemy cloaked as a friend. Predatory lending must be stringently regulated by federal laws that carry prison time if violated.

If we don't, we will be willing participants in creating a nation of paupers!

Chapter 17

The Concept of Not Needing One Another

Cloaked as Personal Independence

—∽∽—

W e have sadly arrived at a place in the long journey of America where people have finally become expendable. We just don't need one another as we once did in times past, and it's evident. Commitment to marriage, family, and friends is at an all-time low. For some, "Till death do us part" is just an empty statement made in a marriage ceremony. The average new marriage in America today lasts nineteen months. That is a national tragedy. If a couple starts to experience difficulty with finances, jobs, or everyday issues of life, they quickly resort to divorce.

I can make it on my own. I don't need you. People have bought into the idea put forth by a secular world that personal independence is best expressed by demonstrating how little we need other people. The steely strength of America has always been the intertwining of people's lives. In the past, it has been the backbone of our social well-being and happiness.

Men today feel they don't need a faithful, nurturing wife and a lifelong companion. Many men see women as objects of sexual gratification, so they move from one to another, using and discarding them. Wives often sit at home alone at night, being ignored by husbands who waste precious togetherness time on useless pursuits. Several have told me, "My husband wants a cook, a housekeeper, an extra paycheck, a mother for his children, and a sex partner; but he doesn't need me." This cavalier attitude is causing women to lose respect and trust for men.

On the other hand, many women feel they don't need men. Fueled by the radical man-hating National Organization for Women and indoctrinated at women's colleges that serve as bastions for anti-man rhetoric, women disdain long-term relationships as unnecessary. One woman told me she bought into that faltering philosophy years ago, and now she is filled with regret that she allowed herself to become hostile and to spurn a number of good men who wanted to share their lives and love with her. Some women adopt children, though they are not married. Others medically have children without a husband, further demonstrating a personal independence that renders the opposite sex obsolete.

Another disturbing trend is found among teens. They suddenly decide Mom and Dad are a meal ticket, a ride, and a place to sleep. But they are, to use their language, so "not relevant." Teens can't seem to wait to get away from the very people who have worked to provide education and care, the people who tended fevered brows at night and sat nervously in emergency rooms while broken bones were set or cuts stitched up. These people cried when their kids were disappointed and laughed when they were happy. They were moms and dads who sacrificed, counted pennies, and did without in order to buy things they couldn't afford so their kids could have material things that other kids had. This detachment from parents is both appalling and sad.

Many older parents never see grown children, never receive a telephone call or a letter. They are left to endure loneliness and weep over pictures of their children from younger days, anguishing over being forgotten by those to whom they gave life, love, and provided a home to grow up in. Some die of loneliness and a broken heart at the realization that they do not mean what they had hoped they would to their children.

My grandparents took me in when I was six months' old, after having reared nine children of their own. I have always been grateful for the love they gave me, and I showed them my love and appreciation as long as they lived. I needed my grandparents, and I knew they needed me. When I said good-bye to them for the last time, I took comfort in knowing that they knew what a wonderful part of my life they had always been.

But too many easily forget the love that was given. This concept of not needing one another is developing a shell around the hearts of our nation's people. A hard shell is fine for M&M's, but not for the human heart. We have always prided ourselves as Americans on the concept of family and friends.

Child abuse in America is our national shame. In a different America, perhaps a Norman Rockwell America, we needed children to make our lives complete and give us added joy. Now children are beaten, molested, tortured, sexually assaulted, and even killed. There is a verse in the Bible that says, ". . . without natural affection." You see, it should be natural for adults to need children, to protect and nurture them. It's unnatural for a man or woman to view children as nuisances, as beings who can be mistreated, knocked around, and exploited. We should possess natural affection for children.

When the national news broke the story of Susan Smith—that her children had been taken along with her car—I knew immediately that she was lying. How did I know so quickly? Human nature of a mother! If you try to take her children away from her, but she loves and needs them, you will leave her either unconscious or dead before you get her kids. Susan Smith didn't have a mark on her. That proved to me that she was coldhearted and did not need or want those two little boys.

It's just natural for the average person to exhibit natural affection. If a child smiling at you doesn't melt your heart, then your heart has become stone. If a sweet, clean, shining, and sleeping small face doesn't bring tears to your eyes, then something is missing inside. If children's laughter does not give you an uplifting feeling, then the milk of human kindness has curdled on your heart.

A civilized society should always love and need children. One of my greatest joys in life was having my sons sleeping securely in my arms or trustingly jumping off the side of a pool to me. I have never felt more needed than when one of my children was sick and the look in their eyes said, *Dad, please make me better.* I am grateful to God that I needed my children and they needed me. Experiencing that mutual need will remain in my memory and my heart forever, and I pray it will be in theirs as well.

My granddaughter Elle is two years old, and she has brought pure joy to my life. When I go to visit her and she sees me, she throws her little arms in the air and shouts, "Grampa!" I pick her up, and she puts her head on my shoulder; I can feel her hand patting my back, and I feel a lump in my throat. I need that child's unconditional and innocent love so very much.

Some parents who would never intentionally mistreat a child physically or verbally just do not understand how to love children. They believe love can be expressed only by constantly providing entertainment or giving material things. The closeness a child experiences from being needed can never be replaced by things.

Studies have proven that the first five years of a child's life will, in a large part, determine many personality traits. Mom and Dad showing their need to hold and love their child will do more to rear a functional and emotionally stable child than anything else. It all flows from needing a child's arms around your neck or that tiny hand in your hand. Children need parents who will need them, really need them, to fill that particular empty space in life that only a child can fill. I will always cherish the privilege to be a dad and the gift of my children. They are men now, married and pursuing careers, but my wife and I still need them; and they continue to need us.

Friendship with other people is a treasure we can place no price on. If we have a true and loyal friend, we are rich indeed. Over the years, I have been privileged to have some wonderful and caring friends who, by their friendships, created a place in my life that added so much joy. I especially remember losing a friend to death. His name was David.

David was the eleventh of eleven children. At thirty years old, he was somewhat mentally slower than others his age, but he had a twinkle in his eye, a song in his heart, and a wonderful sense of humor. I was always amazed at his wisdom about life in general. He made a profound statement once when he said, "You see that man over there? He is smart in one way and a fool in another." I thought,

Wow! What a statement! He did not realize that he had just described a man who is unstable.

When David fell off his bike and struck his head on the pavement, I was called to the hospital and told by the doctor that my friend was gone. To this day, I can still feel the searing hurt that coursed through my heart. David, my friend, was gone, but he would never be forgotten.

So many people define *friend* as someone they can use or someone they can attach themselves to because of personal inadequacies. That's not a friend.

A friend is like my friend Paul. Paul is unassuming. He just likes to go places and do things. We can sit and talk for hours about how life used to be in America or how we wish it were today. He enjoys simple foods and a simple way of living. I can put life's cares to the side for a while and enjoy the presence of an unpretentious friend.

I fear this new independent climate that prevails today has brought forth a new type of friend. It's a friendship that is based solely on mutual interest. In other words, our children are on the same team, so we are friends; we work at the same company, so we are friends. We share the carpooling, so we are friends. If our child changes teams or we change jobs or schools, that mutual interest friendship is many times forgotten. Why? Because we have come to accept the lie that we really don't need friends.

Almost always behind a lack of interest in building a lasting, deep, and abiding friendship is the thinking that we are an island. We are independent, and that is best expressed by not showing how human we are. It will destroy the aura of independence that we have built for ourselves if we demonstrate the long-held belief that having true friends in life is important to our emotional well-being and happiness. A friend is someone who knows all about us, warts and all, but cares for us anyway and will always be there.

Here is something I have never been able to reconcile in my mind. How does a man suddenly decide that he no longer needs his wife and children? He just up and walks out the door and never comes back. To me that is the height of selfishness. Here you have a wife who depends upon her husband to be loyal to her and always be there for her and the kids. She has given him no reason to leave, but he does. Why? Because he wants his independence. He wants to buy the new sports car and be with people who will never add any real love or stability to his life. He is more interested in his independence than in his character and family. His selfishness is only exceeded by his callousness to walk out on children who call him Dad and who will never get over the hurt and rejection they feel.

How does a wife walk out on her husband, a good, caring provider who does everything he can to make her happy? How can she walk out on children she gave birth to? These are children who are a part of her very being, but she leaves them crying for their mother. How can she lust after some fast-talking loser and destroy the family that truly needs her?

My wife and I have been married for thirty-seven years, and I need her as much today as I ever did. Together we have basked in the sunshine on the hills of married life, and we have wept in the deep valleys. It has never crossed our minds not to love and support each other through good times and bad.

I need her smile, her sweet laughter, her encouragement, her kind and gentle way. I could not imagine life without her. I need her to help me dream about the future and to reminisce about the past. I need to know that she truly cares about me—not what I accomplish, but me. I need the love that she has reserved for only me.

I need to take care of her and brush the tears from her cheek. I need to be needed by her. I need to do all I can to bring joy to her life, because she deserves that. I need to reassure her that this long journey we have embarked on together will continue until our time runs out. The need we have had for each other has sustained us and helped us to travel this life's road, knowing we could not do so apart.

Society has taken sides in the commitment or independence debate by providing an easy out for once committed couple. No-fault divorce has made it too easy to choose leaving without guilt rather than working at love and a relationship. The no-fault divorce is a quitter's dream, just made for people who choose to say, "I don't need you," especially when the courts have made it so simple to bail out.

This concept of not needing one another is eroding a stable home life which has been, and always will be, the bedrock of our society. It is just so difficult to understand how the quest for personal independence can so consume some people that they reject needing others or being needed.

335

I had a man tell me that his greatest fear was dying alone with nobody there who needed him or cared if he lived or died. All his life he had never demonstrated that other people mattered or that he ever really needed anybody. He rejected his inner urgings that told him to allow himself to be needed. Now he would die alone, personal independence in tact, but alone. How sad!

Senior citizens are another segment of our society that is no longer needed. After all, what do they have to give? They are old, right? Sometimes their hearing is not as good as it used to be. Maybe their eyesight is not as sharp. Maybe they move slower now than they used to, *but we do need them*. We need their wisdom, for they have been through so much. We need their love, because they are not too busy to give it. We need their companionship, because they are not in a hurry. We need them because they don't put conditions on our relationships, as many others do. We need them because they need us, and their need of us fills an empty void in our lives.

When my grandfather was in a nursing home in the last year of his life, I would go to visit him weekly. He always wanted orange slice candy. Each piece seemed to contain a thousand calories. When he and I sat in the recreation room talking and having orange slice candy, other senior citizens would come into the room. Some looked lonely, and some looked hopeful that they would be asked to join us. Some just looked all alone in the world. Their physical conditions probably did not warrant having the candy, but seeing the joy in their faces as their hands trembled in excited anticipation to get the candy to their mouths was a feeling that only that moment could provide.

I would sit there and listen as an elderly woman talked of her husband who had long since died. She would tell stories of happy days and laugh as if she had never told them before. An elderly man who had retired from working on the railroad talked of old engines and many train trips across America. The stories were very enriching and took me back to a simpler time.

When the nursing home called and told me that my grandfather had passed away, I went to the home and made the necessary arrangements. I kissed his gray head and hugged the other residents. As I walked out into the cold night air and looked up at the stars, I was filled with a sense that I had completed an important part of my purpose on Earth, that of needing and being needed by those who, to the world, maybe seemed useless, but to me were a world of wonderment, love, and joy.

I pray for America! If we lose our need for one another, we will also lose our heart for the whole human race. If we do that, then a nation without a heart will surely wither and die from emotional starvation.

Conclusion

—〰—

America is the most progressive nation on Earth. The advances in technology, industry, medicine, education, and the arts are truly incredible. America is likened to a mighty irresistible force to the rest of the world when it comes to discovering unique ways to better our quality of life. We just continue to march steadily forward, and when it seems we have reached the last pinnacle of invention, we find a new mountain to challenge. Even with all our internal problems, we are still the greatest nation on Earth.

Unfortunately, when we examine ourselves morally, there is a stark contrast. We find ourselves relenting to a particular virulent strain of progressive thinking that has given in to careless actions that are driving us backward on our heels and threaten to force us into moral oblivion. Sadly, morals are not a high priority for self-seekers. I have found that which the heart craves, the heart will get.

We as a people must then accept responsibility for the ultimate destination to which moral absence will deliver us.

We have desired, it seems, everything but a moral direction. Our lusting for money, entertainment, and government's promises to meet all our needs have left us without a reality check of personal incentive for a moral lifestyle in our own personal lives and in our country. This is clearly evident by the proliferation of agenda-driven organizations.

The progression of moral decline comes in phases, and each phase has a cause and effect. In his column, "As I See It," Steve Jarrel wrote, "In 1787 the original thirteen states adopted a new Constitution." Professor Alexander Tyler, a Scottish history professor at the University of Edinburgh, had this to say about the fall of the Athenian republic some two thousand years prior: "A democracy is always temporary in nature. It simply cannot exist as a permanent form of government. A democracy will exist until the time that voters discover that they can vote themselves generous gifts from the public treasury. From that moment on, the majority always votes for the candidates who promise the most benefits from the public treasury, with the result that every democracy will finally collapse due to a loose fiscal policy—which is followed by dictatorship."

Professor Olson of Hamline University School of Law in St. Paul, Minnesota, posted some very interesting and compelling facts about the presidential election between Bush and Gore:

1. Population of counties won by Bush: 143,000,000; Gore: 127,000,000

2. Square miles of land won by Bush: 2,242,700; Gore: 580,000

3. States won by Bush: 29; Gore: 19

4. Murder rate per 100,000 residents in counties won by Bush: 2.1; Gore: 13.2

Professor Olson further adds: "In aggregate the map of the territory Bush won was mostly land owned by the taxpaying citizens of this great country. Gore's territory mostly encompassed those citizens living on government welfare."

Professor Olson believes that America is now somewhere between the complacency and the apathy phases of Professor Tyler's definition of democracy. He further stated that "40 percent of the nation's population has already reached the government dependency phase, and only 51 percent of eligible voters actually voted in the last presidential election" between George Bush and John Kerry.

As you can see, the motivating factor among a large segment of the American people is self-advancement without regard for how they get there. Morals do not enter into the equation. That alone has opened the door for morals to be negated.

Professor Tyler outlined for us where this selfish quest for personal appeasement will lead. He said the following: "The average age of the world's greatest civilizations has been about two hundred years. These nations always progressed through the following sequence — *from bondage to spiritual faith, from spiritual faith to great courage, from great courage to liberty, from liberty to abundance, from abundance to complacency, from complacency to apathy, from apathy to dependence, from dependence back to bondage."*

America's strong and unyielding spiritual faith created a moral willingness to stave off the advance of moral irrelevancy. Our spiritual faith in almighty God and the precepts and principles of Scripture have given us great courage. This great courage that America has always possessed purchased liberty and freedom to live, to worship, and to govern ourselves as a free nation. Realizing that every good thing in life is dependent upon our spiritual faith, we practiced it, and faith brought us God's blessings and abundance.

Now our abundance has made us complacent, and our complacency has allowed these organizations and the monumental issues that I have described in this book to take root in the heart of America. These poisonous roots are wrapping themselves around the life-giving moral standards that have sustained us, and that advancement will choke us to death.

Complacency about the moral condition of America will lead to a dangerous apathy that will ignore the consequences. We will surely become an apathetic populace that is devoid of the fight necessary to stand against these morally defunct hordes. Apathy will result in a weak dependency that will compel us to reach out our hands to the monster that will grind our bones to powder.

Once we become dependent, we will lose our freedom. We will become slaves to wicked and unsound principles that will ensure the demise of our beloved nation and our cherished way of life. We cannot allow those who cloak malice in liberty to deceive us.

May God Almighty give us the good sense to recognize our plight and instill in us the need for spiritual faith that will provide us the resolve to re-claim America before our mighty nation is brought down to an awful and untimely death. *May God help us to do so.*

Acknowledgment

—m—

With special thanks to

Cheryl O'Meara and *LaDonna Harris*

Their hard work and dedication helped to make this book possible.

References and Sources

—ᘒ—

Michael Janofsky - *New York Times*, December 25, 2005

Thomas Sowell - *The State News*

Dr. John Rosemond - *The State News*

Dr. Julian Whitaker - Journal *Health and Healing*

Agape Press

WorldnetDaily.com

Judith Levine – Harmful to Minors: *The Perils of Protecting Children From Sex*

Christian Law Association – *Legal Alert*

Fox News

Public Agenda

The State News (Bill Cosby)

"The O'Reilly Factor"

Henry David Thoreau-Walden

Warren Wiersbe - <u>The Integrity Crisis</u>

George Whitfield – *Whitfield Papers*

Alexis De Tocqueville – *Democracy in America*

Congressional Records

Gallup Poll

Kathleen Parker writing in the *Orlando Sentinel*

John Howard, (Prime minister of Australia)

<u>Koran</u> - Sura 3:79

<u>Wikipedia.com</u>

<u>King James Bible</u>

<u>WordnetDaily.com</u>

Ibrahim Hopper - C.A.I.R.

American Congress for Truth

Investors Business Daily

<u>Koran</u>

Debra Saunders - *Creators Syndicate*

Judge Roy Moore

<u>WorldnetDaily.com</u>

<u>WorldnetDaily.com</u> – Bob Unruh

Ted Sampley - *U.S. Veteran Dispatch*

Gary De Mar - AmericanVision.org

Joseph Wheelan - Jefferson's War: *America's First War on Terror*

WorldnetDaily.com

Arnold Steinberg – *The State News*

Agape Press – *Biblical Evangelist*

Richard Thomas – Thomas More Law Center

Koran, Sura 4: 74 and 76

Former Attorney General Robert Kennedy

Winston Churchhill

Calvin Coolidge – (Former President)

Thomas Jefferson

Russia's Chronicles

Jay Leno – *The Tonight Show*

The State News

Alan Sears, (Former Federal Prosecutor)

Thomas Jefferson, *Danbury Letter*

Patrick Henry

Daniel Webster

Hans Zeiger – Seattle Times, *News With Views*, August 16, 2003

Wall Street Journal, February 1, 1994

Lifenews.com

Benjamin Franklin

Matthew Staver,- *Liberty Journal*

Dick Scarborough – *Vision America*

William Young, *12ᵗʰ U.S. District Court Records*

Dick Lamm – (Former Governor of Colorado)

Benjamin Schwarz – *Atlantic Monthly*

Webster's Dictionary

The Center for Responsible Lending

Post and Courier, August 6, 2007

Steve Jarrel – *As I See It*

Professor Olson – (Hamline University School of Law)

Printed in the United States
117679LV00003B/96/A